go! CHINESE

听说读打写

GO 200

Textbook
(Simplified Character Edition)

罗秋昭   薛意梅
Julie LO   Emily YIH

CENGAGE
Learning™

Australia • Brazil • Japan • Korea • Mexico • Singapore • Spain • United Kingdom • United States

Go! Chinese Go200 Textbook
(Simplified Character Edition)
Julie Lo, Emily Yih

Publishing Director / CLT Product Director:
Paul Tan

Product Manager (Outside Asia):
Mei Yun Loh

Product Manager (Asia):
Joyce Tan

Senior Development Editor:
Lan Zhao

Associate Development Editor:
Coco Koh

Editor:
Cherry Li

Graphic Designer:
Debbie Ng

Assistant Publishing Manager:
Pauline Lim

Senior Publishing Executive:
Gemaine Goh

Marketing Manager (China):
Caroline Ma

Account Manager (China):
Arthur Sun

CLT Coordinator (China):
Mana Wu

Assistant Editor, ELT:
Yuan Ting Soh

ISBN-13: 978-981-4246-44-6
ISBN-10: 981-4246-44-1

Cengage Learning Asia Pte Ltd
5 Shenton Way #01-01
UIC Building
Singapore 068808

Cengage Learning is a leading provider of customized learning solutions with office locations around the globe, including Singapore, the United Kingdom, Australia, Mexico, Brazil, and Japan. Locate your local office at:
www.cengage.com/global

Cengage Learning products are represented in Canada by Nelson Education, Ltd.

For product information, visit **www.cengagesasia.com**

Printed in Singapore
2 3 4 5 13 12 11 10 09

Acknowledgements

Go! Chinese is designed to be used together with *IQChinese Go* courseware, a series of multimedia CD-ROM developed by **IQChinese**. We sincerely thank **Wu, Meng-Tien** (Instruction Manager, IQChinese) and **Lanni Wang** (Instruction Specialist, IQChinese) for their tremendous editorial support and advice throughout the development of this program.

We also like to thank the following individuals who offered many helpful insights, ideas, and suggestions for improvement during the product development stage of *Go! Chinese*.

- **Jessie Lin Brown**, Singapore American School, Singapore
- **Henny Chen**, Moreau Catholic High School, USA
- **Yeafen Chen**, University of Wisconsin-Milwaukee, USA
- **Christina Hsu**, Superior Education, USA
- **Yi Liang Jiang**, Beijing Language and Culture University, China
- **Yan Jin**, Singapore American School, Singapore
- **Kerman Kwan**, Irvine Chinese School, USA
- **Chi-Chien Lu**, IBPS Chinese School, USA
- **Andrew Scrimgeour**, University of South Australia, Australia
- **James L. Tan**, Grace Christian High School, the Philippines
- **Man Tao**, Koning Williem I College, the Netherlands
- **Chiungwen Tsai**, Westside Chinese School, USA
- **Tina Wu**, Westside High School, USA
- **YaWen (Alison) Yang**, Concordian International School, Thailand

Preface

Go! Chinese, together with *IQChinese Go* **multimedia CD-ROM**, is a fully-integrated Chinese language program that offers an easy, enjoyable, and effective learning experience for learners of Chinese as a foreign language.

The themes and lesson plans of the program are designed with reference to the American National Standard for Foreign Language Learning developed by ACTFL[1], and the Curriculum Guides for Modern Languages developed by the Toronto District Board of Education. The program aims to help beginners develop their communicative competence in the four language skills of listening, speaking, reading, and writing while gaining an appreciation of the Chinese culture, exercising their ability to compare and contrast different cultures, making connections with other discipline areas, and extending their learning experiences to their home and communities.

The program employs innovative teaching methodologies and computer applications to enhance language learning, as well as keep students motivated in and outside of the classroom. The CD-ROM companion gives students access to audio, visual, and textual information about the language all at once. Chinese typing is systematically integrated into the program to facilitate the acquisition and retention of new vocabulary and to equip students with a skill that is becoming increasingly important in the Internet era wherein more and more professional and personal correspondence are done electronically.

Course Design

The program is divided into two series: Beginner and Intermediate. The Beginner Series, which comprises four levels (Go100-400), provides a solid foundation for continued study of the Intermediate Series (Go500-800). Each level includes a student text, a workbook, and a CD-ROM companion.

Beginner Series: Go100 – Go400

Designed for zero beginners, each level of the Beginner Series is made up of 10 colorfully illustrated lessons. Each lesson covers new vocabulary and simple sentence structures with particular emphasis on listening and speaking skills. In keeping with the communicative approach, a good mix of activities such as role play, interviews, games, pair work, and language exchanges are incorporated to allow students to learn to communicate through interaction in the target language. The CD-ROM uses rhythmic chants, word games, quizzes, and Chinese typing exercises to improve students' pronunciation, mastery of *pinyin*, and their ability to recognize and read words and sentences taught in each lesson.

The Beginner Series can be completed in roughly 240 hours (160 hours on Textbook and 80 hours on CD-ROM). Upon completion of the Beginner Series, the student will have acquired approximately 500 Chinese characters and 1000 common phrases.

Intermediate Series: Go500 – Go800

The Intermediate Series continues with the use of the communicative approach, but places a greater emphasis on Culture, Community, and Comparison. Through stories revolving around Chinese-American families, students learn vocabulary necessary for expressing themselves in a variety of contexts, describing their world, and discussing cultural differences.

The Intermediate Series can be completed in roughly 320 hours (240 hours on Textbook and 80 hours on CD-ROM). Upon completion of both the Beginner and Intermediate Series, the student will have acquired approximately 1000 Chinese characters and 2400 common phrases.

---

[1] American Council on the Teaching of Foreign Languages (http://www.actfl.org)

Vocabulary and Sentence Structures

The program places emphasis on helping students use the target language in contexts relevant to their everyday lives. Therefore, the chosen vocabulary and sentence structures are based on familiar topics such as family, school activities, hobbies, weather, shopping, food, pets, modes of transport, etc. The same topics are revisited throughout the series to reinforce learning, as well as to expand on the vocabulary and sentence structures acquired before.

Listening and Speaking

Communicative activities encourage and require a learner to speak with and listen to other learners. Well-designed and well-executed communicative activities can help turn the language classroom into an active and enjoyable place where learners are motivated to learn and can learn what they need. The program integrates a variety of communicative activities such as role play, interviews, games, pair work, and language exchanges to give students the opportunity to put what they have learned into practice.

Word Recognition and Reading

Each lesson introduces about 12 new Chinese characters. Using the spiral approach, each new character is first introduced and then recycled in classroom activities and subsequent lessons to enhance retention of new vocabulary over time. *Pinyin* (phonetic notation) is added above newly introduced characters so that students can learn to pronounce them. To make sure students do not become over-reliant on *pinyin* to read Chinese, recycled vocabulary is stripped of *pinyin* so that students can learn to recognize and read the actual written characters in due course. For the same reason, the CD-ROM companion does not display the *pinyin* of words automatically.

Type-to-Learn Methodology

The unique characteristic of this series is the use of Chinese typing as an instructional strategy to improve listening, pronunciation, and word recognition. Activities in the CD-ROM require students to type characters or sentences as they are read aloud or displayed on the computer screen. Students will be alerted if they make a mistake and will be given the chance to correct them. If they don't get it on the third try, the software provides immediate feedback on how to correct the error. This interactive trial-and-error process allows students to develop self-confidence and learn the language by doing.

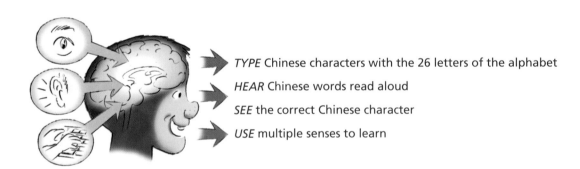

TYPE Chinese characters with the 26 letters of the alphabet

HEAR Chinese words read aloud

SEE the correct Chinese character

USE multiple senses to learn

Chinese Characters and Character Writing

The program does not require the student to be able to hand-write all the core vocabulary; the teacher may however assign more character writing practice according to his or her classroom emphasis and needs. What the program aims to do is to give students a good grasp of Chinese radicals and stroke order rules, as well as to help students understand and appreciate the characteristics and formation of Chinese characters. The program includes writing practice on frequently used characters. Understanding the semantic function radicals have in the characters they form and having the ability to see compound characters by their simpler constituents enable students to memorize new characters in a logical way.

Using the CD-ROM as an Instructional Aid

The following diagram shows how a teacher might use the CD-ROM as an instructional aid to improve traditional classroom instruction.

Textbook   *Multimedia CD-ROM*

Segment 1
(1st class hour)

WARM-UP
Arouse students' interest and set the tone for the whole lesson

Get Started—Additional topic-related words to expand students' vocabulary for daily conversation

Text > Chant

Segment 2
(2nd class hour)

Let's **CHANT**
Rhyming text to be read aloud

Drill > Word Builder

Drill > Sentence Builder

Segment 3
(3rd class hour)

Let's Learn **GRAMMAR**
Grammar

Text > Sentence Pattern

Segment 4
(4th class hour)

Exercise > Word Game

Let's **TALK**
Scripted dialogue practice that may be extended or modified

Text > Dialogue

Let's Learn **CHARACTER**   Let's Learn **PUNCTUATION**
Learn about Chinese characters and punctuation

Segment 5
(5th class hour)

Exercise > Sentence Quiz #

Let's **READ**
Reading and comprehension

Text > Reading

Segment 6
(6th class hour)

Let's **DO IT**
Review and reinforcement activities

LEARNING LOG
Conclusion and students' self-evaluation

#Sentence Quiz Exercise

The section *Exercise > Sentence Quiz* in the CD-ROM enhances learning by stimulating multiple senses as well as providing immediate feedback on students' performance.

The Sentence Quiz exercise comprises four levels.

- Level 1 – Warm-up Quiz (Look, Listen, and Type): Chinese text, *pinyin*, and audio prompts are provided.

- Level 2 – Visual-aid Quiz: Only Chinese text is provided. There are no *pinyin* or audio prompts.

- Level 3 – Audio-aid Quiz: Only audio prompts are provided.

- Level 4 – Character-selection Quiz: Only Chinese text is provided. After entering the correct *pinyin*, students are required to select the correct character from a list of similar-looking characters.

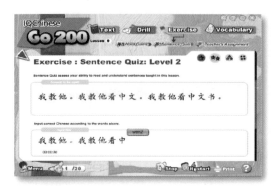

Typing practice for important sentences in every lesson reinforces the connection between words and sounds, and helps students to identify words better.

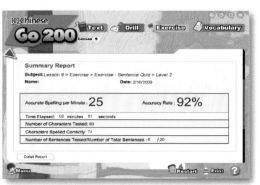

Summary Report reveals immediately students' accuracy rate and speed of typing per minute.

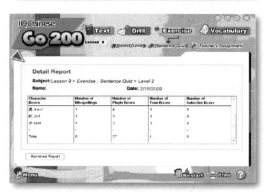

Detail Report lists characters typed erroneously three times during the quiz. It also shows details of errors based on categories such as *pinyin*, tone, and word selection. The instant feedback feature enables students to make self-improvement right away.

Classroom Setup and Equipment

For small classes (up to 5 students), the teacher can show the features of the CD-ROM on one computer with her students gathered around the screen. For large groups, a projector will be needed to project the computer's display onto a large screen so that the entire class can see.

If the classroom is not equipped with computers, the teacher may have students bring their own portable computers to class so that they can work individually or in small groups of 2 to 3 on the CD-ROM activities during designated class hours. She may also assign CD-ROM activities as homework.

Suggestions for Teachers

We recommend that the teacher

- spend 4-5 hours on each lesson in the Textbook and 2 hours on each lesson in the CD-ROM. The course materials and lesson length may be adjusted according to students' proficiency level and learning ability.
- allocate 1-2 class hours to go over with her students the Review units in the Workbook as a way to check on the students' progress.
- have her students complete 1-2 pages of the Workbook after every two class sessions.
- encourage her students to spend 10 minutes a day on the Sentence Quiz in the CD-ROM. Practice makes perfect!

For detailed chapter-by-chapter lesson plans, teaching slides, and supplementary assignments, please refer to one of the following websites:

Cengage Learning http://www.cengageasia.com

IQChinese http://www.iqchinese.com

Scope & Sequence

Lesson	Communicative Goals	Vocabulary	Language Usage	Cultural Information
我去上学 Going to School **1**	• Use basic verbs "wear", "put on", and "take" appropriately • Indicate tense in Chinese	**Getting ready for school** 穿, 戴, 拿, 帽子, 鞋, 书包, 去, 上学, 看见, 说, 背, 书…	• **Parts of one's clothing and the appropriate verb to use for each** 我穿鞋子。 • **Indicating tense in Chinese** 我要戴帽子。 我在戴帽子。 • **Sentence pattern "看见……了吗?"** 你看见我的书包了吗? • **Sequence of writing Chinese characters—from top to bottom** • **Chinese characters that are vertically long**	• Traditional costumes of different countries
我有什么? **What Do I Have?** **2**	• Accurately use measure words to describe or ask about the quantity of objects • Talk about what I have	**Describing quantity** 张, 本, 支, 台, 笔, 白纸, 问, 问题, 回答, 里, 杯子, 电脑…	• **Sentence pattern "有几(支)……?"** 你有几支笔? 我有十支笔。/ 我没有笔。 • **Usage of "来 / 去"** 星期日你来我家, 好不好? 星期日我去你家。 • **Usage of "问"** 我问老师一个问题。 • **Usage of Chinese punctuation "。" and ", "** 我的书包里有两支笔, 还有七张纸。	
什么样儿? **What Does Everything Look Like?** **3**	• Describe the appearance of people or objects • Describe the location of objects with the prepositions "above", "under", and "inside"	**Describing appearance** 方, 圆, 高, 矮, 胖, 瘦, 长, 短, 桌子, 椅子, 句子, 上, 下, 样儿, 一样, 字…	• **Usage of "上 / 下 / 里"** 桌子上有一支笔。 桌子下有一个背包。 书包里有两本书。 • **Sentence patterns "看到……有…… / 看到……在……"** 我看到桌子上有两本书。 我看到书在桌子上。 • **Sentence pattern "有……, 有的……, 有的……"** 人有胖瘦, 有的胖, 有的瘦。 • **Reduplication of adjectives** 圆 → 圆圆的 • **Sequence of writing Chinese characters—from left to right** • **Chinese characters with a thin left component and a wide right component**	• The significance of a circle in Chinese culture

Lesson	Communicative Goals	Vocabulary	Language Usage	Cultural Information
多看多听 Look More & Listen More **4**	• Use appropriate measure words to talk about my sense organs and limbs • Talk about the uses of my sense organs and limbs	**Uses of my sense organs and limbs** 眼睛, 嘴, 耳朵, 手, 多, 做, 做事, 听, 忘, 只, 双, 打字…	• Sentence pattern "我有……，我用……" 我有眼睛，我用眼睛看。 • Sentence pattern "是……的" 这台电脑是哥哥的。 • Usage of adverb "多" 我们要多看、多学、多做事。 • Sequence of writing Chinese characters—horizontal strokes before vertical strokes • Chinese characters with "口" as the left component	
我吃什么? What Do I Eat? **5**	• Name common foodstuff • Ask about others' dietary preference or indicate my own preference • Express the fact that an action has been completed	**Food and drink** 吃, 喝, 早上, 牛奶, 面包, 果汁, 三明治, 饭, 菜, 也, 吃饱, 够, 早饭…	• Sentence patterns "要（吃）……吗? / 吃不吃？" 你要吃面包吗? 你吃不吃饭? • Sentence patterns "要……，还要…… / 要……，也要……" 我要吃面包，还要喝牛奶。 我要吃面包，也要喝牛奶。 • Usage of "了" 早上我吃了三明治。	• The significance of eating in Chinese culture • Evolution of Chinese characters
走路开车 Walking & Driving **6**	• Remind others of road safety • Use prepositions of location to indicate the position of objects	**Positions and traffic** 上面, 下面, 左边, 右边, 前面, 后面, 走路, 开车, 小心, 红灯, 就是, 停, 绿灯…	• Sentence pattern "（一）……，就……" （一）看见红灯，我就停。 • Usage of "就是" 他就是王老师。 • Reduplication of verbs 走 → 走一走 / 走走 • Reduplication of prepositions of location 上下 → 上上下下 • Sequence of writing Chinese characters—writing the bottom stroke last for fully framed characters • Partially framed Chinese characters	• Traffic signals and road orientation may differ in different countries.
我玩游戏 Playing Games **7**	• Use five common colors to describe objects • Talk about a favorite game or activity • Describe the location of an activity • Ask others if they would like to engage in a certain activity	**Colors and games** 白色, 黑色, 蓝色, 红色, 绿色, 蓝天, 白云, 打球, 天气, 散步, 绿草地, 玩, 游戏, 爱…	• Sentence pattern "在……" 哥哥在家里吃饭。 • Usage of "好不好？" 我们一起去打球，好不好? • Usage of "爱" 爸爸爱散步。 • Reduplication of verbs 打球 → 打打球 • Usage of Chinese punctuation "？" and "！" 请问现在几点钟? 天是蓝的，云是白的，天气很好!	• Traditional children's games in China

Lesson	Communicative Goals	Vocabulary	Language Usage	Cultural Information
春夏秋冬 The Four Seasons **8**	• Describe the different sceneries of the four seasons • Talk about common activities that take place in different seasons	**The four seasons** 种花, 除草, 扫落叶, 铲雪, 春天, 花, 夏天, 草, 秋天, 落叶, 雪, 冬天...	• **Sentence pattern "有时……，有时……"** 春天到了，有时妈妈种花，有时弟弟种花。 • **Sentence pattern "除了……，还有……"** 桌子上，除了笔，还有三本书。 • **Usage of "都"** 秋天，叶子都落了。 • **Chinese characters with a light top component and a heavy bottom component**	• Seasons, the agricultural system, and the lunar calendar • Evolution of Chinese characters
我的妈妈 My Mother **9**	• Describe the chores performed by members of my family • Express my perspective on things around me • Describe the multiple things that a person has to do	**Life as a family (doing household chores)** 衣服, 洗, 写字, 功课, 真, 辛苦, 做饭, 幸福...	• **Sentence pattern "……好了吗？"** 你扫好了吗？还没，我还没扫好。 • **Sentence pattern "要……，还要……"** 姐姐要洗衣服，还要做饭。 • **Usage of adverb "真"** 你的帽子真好看。 • **Sequence of writing Chinese characters—left-falling stroke before right-falling stroke**	
我的爸爸 My Father **10**	• Introduce my family • Talk about one's ability to do something • Convey a continuous time frame	**Life as a family** 上班, 下班, 接, 送, 能, 能干, 赚钱, 照顾, 每天, 忙, 从, 又...	• **Sentence patterns "能 / 不能 / 能……吗？ / 能不能？"** 哥哥能写二百个中文字。 今天天气不好，我不能去散步。 我能去打球吗？ 我能不能去找小明？ • **Sentence pattern "从……到……"** 妈妈从早到晚都很忙。 • **Sentence pattern "又……，又……"** 爸爸又要扫地，又要做饭。 • **Sequence of writing Chinese characters—writing the radical "辶" last** • **Chinese characters with a heavy top component and a light bottom component**	

Table of Contents

我去上学
Going to School

My Goals

1 Accurately use common verbs such as "wear", "put on", "take", "carry", "see", "say", and "go" in Chinese
2 Understand the usage of tense in verbs in Chinese
3 Understand the principle of writing from top to bottom when writing Chinese characters
4 Become familiar with vocabulary associated with clothing

Get Started

shǒu tào
手套
(gloves)

shǒu biǎo
手表
(watch)

mào zi
帽子
(hat)

yǎn jìng
眼镜
(glasses)

wà zi
袜子
(socks)

xié zi
鞋子
(shoes)

kù zi
裤子
(pants)

yī fu
衣服
(clothes)

⭐ Identify It

Can you tell which countries the following traditional costumes represent?

⭐ Think and Answer

What items can "穿", "戴", and "拿" be used with?

New Words

chuān
穿 wear, dressed in (socks, dress, suit, etc.)

dài
戴 wear, put on (gloves, accessories, etc.)

ná
拿 take

Let's CHANT

dài   mào zi chuān   xié
戴上帽子穿上鞋，

ná   shū bāo   qù shàng xué
我拿书包去上学，

kàn jiàn   shuō shēng
看见老师说声早，

kàn jiàn   shuō shēng
看见同学说声好。

TIP "去" may be used before or after another verb. "去 + verb" indicates an upcoming action, for example, "去上学" (go to school).

New Words

mào zi 帽子 hat	xié 鞋 shoes	shū bāo 书包 school bag, backpack	qù 去 go to
shàng xué 上学 go to school	kàn jiàn 看见 see	shuō 说 say, speak	shēng 声 voice

Let's Learn GRAMMAR

New Words

bēi
背 carry (on the back)

shū
书 book

bēi bāo
背包 backpack

| 我 | chuān 穿 | xié zi 鞋子。 |
| | bēi 背 | shū bāo 书包。 |

哥哥	chuān 穿	xié zi 鞋子
姐姐	dài 戴	mào zi 帽子
弟弟	bēi 背	shū bāo 书包
妹妹	ná 拿	shū 书
他	dǎ 打	电话

bēi bāo
背包

Tenses in Chinese

dài mào zi
我戴帽子。

dài mào zi
我要戴帽子。

dài mào zi
我在戴帽子。

dài mào zi qù shàng xué
我戴上帽子去上学。

TIP Chinese and English are different in expressing tense—in Chinese, the verb stays unchanged while adverbs, phrases indicating time and aspectual particles (which indicate whether an action is ongoing, recently completed, or completed long ago) are added to indicate the progress of an action.

In the examples on the left, "我戴帽子" is to state a fact; "要戴" is to express a desire, indicating that the action (戴) has not taken place yet; "在戴" expresses a state of an action and indicates that the action (戴) is taking place now; "戴上" indicates that the action (戴) has been completed, but the clause (我戴上帽子) should be followed by further information to complete the sentence.

你　看见　我的　书包　了吗？
（kàn jiàn）（shū bāo）

你看见弟弟的帽子了吗？
（kàn jiàn）（mào zi）

你看见爸爸的帽子了吗？
（kàn jiàn）（mào zi）

TIP The younger brother has seen his sister's backpack. To indicate that the action "看见" is over, "了" is added to the end of the sentence.

哥哥说："你看见妹妹的背包了吗？"
（shuō）（kàn jiàn）（bēi bāo）

弟弟说："我看见妹妹的背包了。"
（shuō）（kàn jiàn）（bēi bāo）

小明说："你看见我的鞋子了吗？"
（shuō）（kàn jiàn）（xié zi）

大关说："我没（有）看见你的鞋子。"
（shuō）（kàn jiàn）（xié zi）

TIP "我没看见你的鞋子。" and "我没有看见你的鞋子。" mean the same. In verbal speech, "没" is commonly used alone; the accompanying "有" may be omitted.

Ⓐ：你看见哥哥的书了吗？
（kàn jiàn）（shū）

B1：我看见了。
（kàn jiàn）

B2：我没（有）看见。
（kàn jiàn）

Go200

WANT TO LEARN MORE?

Check out the Text > Sentence Pattern section in the Go200 CD.

Find a partner and practice the following dialogues.

⭐ Task 1

Ⓐ: 妈妈，你看见我的帽子了吗？
kàn jiàn mào zi

Ⓑ: 没有，我没看见。
kàn jiàn

Ⓐ: 爸爸，你看见我的帽子了吗？
kàn jiàn mào zi

Ⓒ: 没有。这是谁的帽子？
mào zi

Ⓐ: 那是妹妹的帽子。
mào zi

⭐ Task 2

: 你有帽子吗？
mào zi

: 我＿＿＿＿＿＿＿。

: 你有书吗？
shū

: 我＿＿＿＿＿＿＿。

⭐ Task 3

Ⓐ： 你拿什么？
<small>ná</small>

Ⓑ： 我拿书包。
<small>ná shū bāo</small>

Ⓐ： 你拿书包去哪里(where)？
<small>ná shū bāo qù nǎ lǐ</small>

Ⓑ： 我拿书包去同学家。
<small>ná shū bāo qù</small>

Ⓐ： 妹妹，你背书包去哪里？
<small>bēi shū bāo qù nǎ lǐ</small>

Ⓒ： 我背书包去上学。
<small>bēi shū bāo qù shàng xué</small>

TIP

"去 + location" indicates a change in location —from the speaker's present location to another.

⭐ Task 4

Ⓐ： 看见老师，你说什么？
<small>kàn jiàn　　　　shuō</small>

Ⓑ： 我说"＿＿＿＿＿＿。"
<small>shuō</small>

Ⓐ： 看见同学，你说什么？
<small>kàn jiàn　　　　shuō</small>

Ⓑ： 我说"＿＿＿＿＿＿。"
<small>shuō</small>

The following dialogues are adapted from the dialogues in your  Go 200. You may listen to the CD before reading the transcript on this page.

⭐ Task 5

A: 明天你去不去？
qù   qù

B: 明天我不去。
qù

⭐ Task 6

A: 你几点去上学？
qù shàng xué

B: 我早上八点半去上学。
qù shàng xué

⭐ Task 7

A: 这是谁的帽子？
mào zi

B: 这是我的帽子。
mào zi

> To answer a question with "谁", you do not need to change the sentence structure of your answer but simply replace "谁" in the sentence with your answer.

A: 你看见我的帽子了吗？
kàn jiàn   mào zi

B: 我没（有）看见。
kàn jiàn

Go 200

WANT TO LEARN MORE?

Check out the Text > Dialogue section in the Go200 CD.

Let's Learn CHARACTER

⭐ Sequence of Writing Chinese Characters

From Top to Bottom

Chinese characters are composed of eight basic strokes which are written in a particular order. Writing the strokes in their order not only makes for beautiful calligraphy, but also makes it easier for one to remember how a character is written. In this lesson, we introduce a method of calligraphy in which we write the strokes from top to bottom.

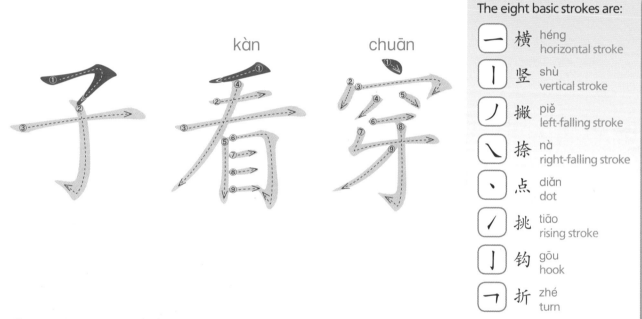

kàn   chuān

The eight basic strokes are:		
一	横	héng horizontal stroke
丨	竖	shù vertical stroke
丿	撇	piě left-falling stroke
乀	捺	nà right-falling stroke
丶	点	diǎn dot
╱	挑	tiāo rising stroke
亅	钩	gōu hook
㇕	折	zhé turn

⭐ Structure of Chinese Characters

Characters that are Vertically Long

In the evolution from illustrations to the standard modern form, Chinese characters have always been composed of linear strokes. Nonetheless, there is a great variety in the structure and appearance of individual Chinese characters. Paying attention to the structure and appearance of Chinese characters will enhance your appreciation of the language. In Chinese, characters which are vertically long in their structure are very common. This lesson introduces you to three of such characters.

kàn

Read the following text carefully.

星期一到星期五，早上九点钟，我和姐姐

qù shàng xué　　　ná　shū bāo　　ná　shū bāo　　dài

一起去上学。她拿大书包，我拿小书包，她戴

mào zi　　　dài mào zi　　　　　　　qù shàng xué

大帽子，我不戴帽子，我们一起去上学。

Answer these questions in Chinese.

1　How many days in a week do they not go to school?
2　Who is carrying a big school bag and wearing a big hat?
3　Is the author wearing a hat? Is he carrying a school bag?

Text 2

Read the following text carefully.

今天星期一，早上七点三十分，我和姐姐

_{chuān xié zi dài mào zi}
穿上鞋子，戴上帽子，我们一起去上学。弟弟 _{qù shàng xué}

_{kàn jiàn shuō}
看见了，他说："我要和你们一起去。"妈妈 _{qù}

_{duì shuō}
对弟弟说*："你太小了*，不可以去上学。"我 _{tài xiǎo le qù shàng xué}

_{duì shuō}
对弟弟说："明年你七岁，你背小书包，我背 _{bēi shū bāo bēi}

_{shū bāo qù shàng xué}
大书包，我们一起去上学。"

* 对……说 say something to someone

* 太小了 too young

Answer these questions in Chinese.

1 How did the author dress himself up for school?
2 Did the author's younger brother want to go to school?
3 Why couldn't the author's younger brother go to school?
4 According to the text, how old must one be to go to school?

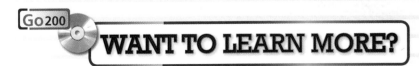

WANT TO LEARN MORE?

Check out the Text > Reading section in the Go200 CD.

1   Form a group of four members and stand in a row.

2   The first student is to go to the teacher for a message (a sentence that associated with one of the four pictures above), memorize it, and repeat it to the second student behind him. The students should speak softly so that others will not hear the message.

3   The second student will relay the message to the third student, and so on. Once the last student has received the message, he has to write the message on the blackboard as well as state which picture his message matches. The team which does it the fastest, and with the most accurate and complete final message wins.

4   Upon completion of the game, choose any two messages and write them in the table below.

①

②

LEARNING LOG

I can...	Excellent	Good	Fair	Needs Improvement
1 label the clothes that I am wearing in Chinese.	☐	☐	☐	☐
2 use "穿", "戴", and "拿" respectively on appropriate items.	☐	☐	☐	☐
3 use "我要穿……", "我在穿……", and "我穿上……" appropriately.	☐	☐	☐	☐
4 write Chinese characters from top to bottom.	☐	☐	☐	☐
5 write "穿", "背", "去", "看", and "说".	☐	☐	☐	☐

我有什么？
What Do I Have?

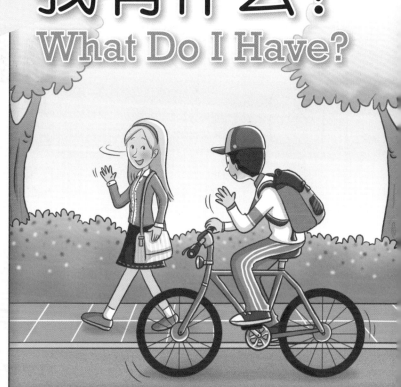

My Goals

1 Accurately use measure words "张", "本", "支", and "台"
2 Competently state and ask questions about the quantity of items
3 Become familiar with Chinese punctuation " , " and " 。"
4 Become familiar with vocabulary associated with stationery

	书包	
个	学生	
	bēi zi 杯子 (cup)	
zhāng 张	zhǐ 纸 (paper)	
	chuáng 床 (bed)	
	zhuō zi 桌子 (table)	
běn 本	书	
zhī 支	bǐ 笔 (pen)	
tái 台	diàn nǎo 电脑 (computer)	

Describe It

In the format of "number + measure word + item", read out the items in the table above.

New Words

zhāng
张 (a measure word used for flat, sheet-like items)

běn
本 (a measure word used for books, parts of a series, etc.)

zhī
支 (a measure word used for long, thin, inflexible objects)

tái
台 (a measure word used for computers)

zhī bǐ
一个书包两支笔，

zhāng bái zhǐ   běn
三张白纸四本书，

wèn wèn tí
五个学生问问题，

huí dá
六个老师来回答。

TIP

"来" may be used before or after another verb. "来 + verb" indicates an upcoming action.

New Words

bǐ 笔 pen	bái zhǐ 白纸 blank paper	wèn 问 ask
wèn tí 问题 question	huí dá 回答 answer	

Let's Learn GRAMMAR

你 有 | 几支笔 ?
zhī bǐ

lǐ *běn*
书包里有几本书?

zhǐ bēi
你有几个纸杯 (paper cup) ?

我	有	十支 *zhī*	笔 *bǐ* 。
	没有		

lǐ *běn*
书包里有四本书。

zhǐ bēi
我没有纸杯。

Ⓐ: 你家有几台电脑?
tái diàn nǎo

Ⓑ1: 我家有两台电脑。
tái diàn nǎo

Ⓑ2: 我家没有电脑。
diàn nǎo

Want More Practice?

Fit the following words into the sentence structures on this page to form new sentences.

书包   白纸   杯子
bái zhǐ *bēi zi*

桌子   本子
zhuō zi *běn zi*
(notebook)

电脑
diàn nǎo

In describing quantities, we do not add measure words after "没有".

来 / 去

Ⓐ： 明天下午三点，你和
你弟弟可以来我家吗？

Ⓑ： 明天下午三点，我和
弟弟一起去你家。

Ⓐ： 星期日你来我家，好不
好？

Ⓑ： 好。星期日我去你家。

TIP
You can add a verb or location after "来" and "去".

➤ A verb after "来" or "去" indicates an upcoming action.

➤ "来 + location" indicates a movement from somewhere else to where the speaker is now. For example, "我来学^{xué}校^{xiào}看书。" indicates that the speaker is already at his school.

➤ "去 + location" indicates a movement from where the speaker is to another location. For example, "我要去学校^{xué xiào}。" indicates that the speaker is not at his school yet, but will go there later.

问 ^{wèn}

TIP
When asking someone for help on a query, you may add a name or your question after the verb "问".

我问^{wèn}问题^{wèn tí}。

我问^{wèn}老师一个问题^{wèn tí}。   妹妹问^{wèn}妈妈现在几点钟？

Go 200
WANT TO LEARN MORE?

Check out the Text > Sentence Pattern section in the Go200 CD.

Task 1

Find a partner and practice the dialogue below.

一 + ? + 书

Ⓐ: 我有^{wèn}问^{tí}题，可以^{wèn}问老师吗？

Ⓑ: 可以，你要^{wèn}问什么？

Ⓐ: 请^{wèn}问老师，我可以说"我有一个书。"吗？

Ⓑ: 不可以。你要说"我有一^{běn}本书。"

Task 2

Work out the answers with your partner and practice the dialogue below.

Ⓐ: 你的书包^{lǐ}里有几^{běn}本书？

Ⓑ: 我的书包^{lǐ}里有＿＿＿＿＿＿。

Ⓐ: 你的书包^{lǐ}里还有什么？

Ⓑ: 我的书包^{lǐ}里有＿＿＿＿，还有＿＿＿＿。

Ⓐ: 我的书包^{lǐ}里有＿＿＿＿＿。

Find a partner and practice the following dialogues.

★ **Task 3**

Ⓐ: 你买什么？

Ⓑ: 我买三本书。
bĕn

Ⓐ: 你买什么书？

Ⓑ: 我买＿＿＿＿＿＿。

★ **Task 4**

Ⓐ: 你有几支笔？
zhī bǐ

Ⓑ: 我有十支笔。
zhī bǐ

Ⓐ: 你有白纸吗？
bái zhǐ

Ⓑ: 有，我有白纸。
bái zhǐ

Ⓐ: 请问你有几张白纸？
wèn   zhāng bái zhǐ

Ⓑ: 我有八张白纸。
zhāng bái zhǐ

Ⓐ: 你拿白纸做什么？
bái zhǐ zuò shén me

Ⓑ: 我拿白纸来写字。
bái zhǐ   xiě zì

> "做什么" is a common phrase used to ask for a purpose.

The following dialogues are adapted from the dialogues in your . You may listen to the CD before reading the transcript on this page.

⭐Task 5

Ⓐ : 你会回答这个问题吗？
<small>huí dá · · · · wèn tí</small>

Ⓑ : 不会，我不会回答，请你教我。
<small>huí dá</small>

Ⓐ : 你会回答这个问题吗？
<small>huí dá · · · · wèn tí</small>

Ⓒ : 会，我会回答。
<small>huí dá</small>

⭐Task 6

你有没有问题？
<small>wèn tí</small>

我有一个问题。
<small>wèn tí</small>

你有什么问题？
<small>wèn tí</small>

_____？

这个问题我不会，谁来回答这个问题？
<small>wèn tí · · · · huí dá · · · · wèn tí</small>

我来回答。
<small>huí dá</small>

Go 200

WANT TO LEARN MORE?

Check out the Text > Dialogue section in the Go200 CD.

Let's Learn
PUNCTUATION

jù hào
句号
(period)

Once you have finished a sentence, write a small circle "。", indicating that your sentence is complete. In English, a period is a small dot but in Chinese, a period is represented by a small circle.

我有两个妹妹。

huí dá wèn tí
我来回答问题。

dòu hào
逗号
(comma)

When a sentence is incomplete but requires a pause, use a comma " , ". When the sentence is complete, use a period "。" to indicate that that is the end of the sentence.

běn
这九本书，一共十五块五。

早上我戴上帽子，穿上鞋子，
和哥哥一起去上学。

> "十五块五" means
> 15 dollars and 50 cents.
> In some places, people say
> "十五块半".

Practice It

Fill in the blanks with the correct punctuation marks.

zhāng bái zhǐ   bēi zi
① 弟弟有两张白纸◯还有五个杯子◯

② 我和同学一起学中文◯

Text 1  Go 200

Read the following text carefully.

zhī bǐ
两支笔，一块钱，

bēi zi
一个杯子，一块三，

běn běn zi
一本本子*，一块半，

běn
一本书，十块钱，

一个书包，十八块钱，

zhōng
一个钟*，一百块钱。

wèn
请问一共多少钱？

> TIP
> The phrase "一本本子" is composed of the measuring phrase "一本" and the noun "本子". Therefore, in reading aloud, remember to read the phrase as 一本 本子.

*本子 notebook

*钟 clock

Answer these questions in Chinese.

1 How much are two books? How much is a pen?

2 How much would it cost to buy one of each item?

3 Arrange the items from the most expensive to the least expensive in the boxes below.

Text 2

Read the following text carefully.

我们上中文课*，老师教我们说中文。
^{kè}

老师说杯子要一个一个算，我们要说一个
^{bēi zi}

杯子、两个杯子；纸要一张一张算，我们要说
^{bēi zi} ^{bēi zi} ^{zhǐ} ^{zhāng} ^{zhāng}

一张纸、两张纸；书要一本一本算，我们要说
^{zhāng zhǐ} ^{zhāng zhǐ} ^{běn} ^{běn}

一本书、两本书；笔要一支一支算，我们要说
^{běn} ^{běn} ^{bǐ} ^{zhī} ^{zhī}

一支笔、两支笔；电脑要一台一台算，我们要
^{zhī bǐ} ^{zhī bǐ} ^{diàn nǎo} ^{tái} ^{tái}

说一台电脑、两台电脑。
^{tái diàn nǎo} ^{tái diàn nǎo}

今天我们学会很多中文。

* 中文课 Chinese lesson

Answer these questions in Chinese.

1 What lesson did they attend today?
2 How did they count the cups, the pieces of paper, and the book?
3 What else can you quantify with "个" apart from cups? What else can you quantify with "张" apart from paper?

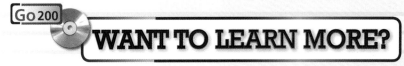

Check out the Text > Reading section in the Go200 CD.

我有什么？   23

Let's DO IT

Imagine that your community has organized an auction. How do you bid for something that you wish to buy?

1. Students draw lots to decide what they get to purchase in the activity, then they throw dice to determine the quantity that they will buy.

2. Work in pairs. One of you will pretend to be the sales assistant while the other will be the customer. Complete the following transaction and record your transaction details.

Sales Assistant : 请问你要买什么？
wèn

Customer : 请问书包多少钱？
wèn

Sales Assistant : 一个书包十五块，请问你要买几个？
wèn

Customer : _____

Sales Assistant : _____

个　张　支
zhāng　*zhī*

本　台
běn　*tái*

LEARNING LOG

I can...

		Excellent	Good	Fair	Needs Improvement
1	name my stationery to my friends.	☐	☐	☐	☐
2	use the appropriate measure words to request for quantities of specific items.	☐	☐	☐	☐
3	use measure words such as "本", "个", "张", "支", and "台" to indicate the quantity of items.	☐	☐	☐	☐
4	use a comma " , " for a pause when a sentence is incomplete, and a period "。" when the sentence is complete.	☐	☐	☐	☐
5	write "纸", "笔", "支", "答", and "回".	☐	☐	☐	☐

24　我有什么？

什么样儿？
What Does Everything Look Like?

My Goals

1 Use adjectives to describe the appearance of people and objects
2 Describe the location of an object
3 Use reduplication of adjectives to describe something
4 Understand the principle of writing from left to right when writing Chinese characters
5 Become familiar with vocabulary to describe the physical appearance of people and things

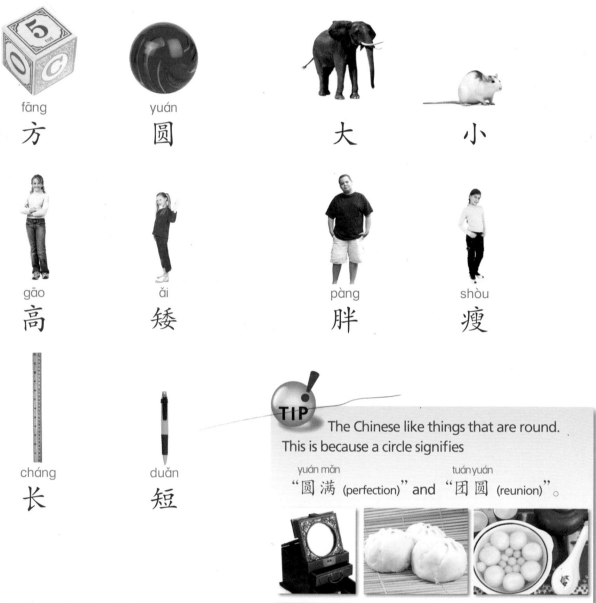

fāng
方

yuán
圆

大

小

gāo
高

ǎi
矮

pàng
胖

shòu
瘦

cháng
长

duǎn
短

TIP

The Chinese like things that are round. This is because a circle signifies

yuán mǎn
tuán yuán

"圆满 (perfection)" and "团圆 (reunion)"。

Describe It

To a partner, describe people or objects in the classroom using the words you see above. How many people or objects can you describe in Chinese?

New Words

fāng	yuán	gāo	ǎi	pàng	shòu	cháng	duǎn
方	圆	高	矮	胖	瘦	长	短
square	round	tall	short	fat	thin	long	short

zhuō zi fāng　　yǐ　zi yuán
桌子方，椅子圆。

rén yǒu pàng shòu yǒu gāo ǎi
人有胖瘦有高矮。

zì yǒu dà　　zì yǒu xiǎo
字有大，字有小。

jù　zi　chángduǎn
书里句子有长短。

New Words

zhuō zi
桌子 table

yǐ　zi
椅子 chair

jù　zi
句子 sentence

zì
字 word; letter; character

Let's Learn GRAMMAR

上 / 下 / 里
shàng xià

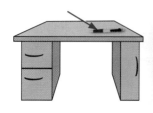

桌子上
zhuō zi shàng

桌子上有一支笔。
zhuō zi shàng

书包里

书包里有两本书。

桌子下
zhuō zi xià

桌子下有一个背包。
zhuō zi xià

我	看到 kàn dào	桌子上 zhuō zi shàng	有	两本书。

小明看到书包里有五张白纸。
kàn dào

我	看到 kàn dào	书	在	桌子上。 zhuō zi shàng

哥哥看到书包在椅子下。
kàn dào yǐ zi xià

> These two sentence structures may appear similar, but the emphasis in each sentence is actually different. The emphasis in the first sentence is on the object (两本书), while the emphasis in the second sentence is on the location (桌子上).

New Words

上 shàng up; above	下 xià down; under	看到 kàn dào saw

28   什么样儿?

| 人
zì
字 | 有 | pàng shòu
胖瘦，
大小， | 有的 | pàng
胖，
大， | 有的 | shòu
瘦。
小。 |

gāo ǎi   gāo
人有高矮，有的（人）高，

ǎi
有的（人）矮。

zhuō zi   fāng yuán   zhuō zi   fāng
桌子有方圆，有的（桌子）方，

zhuō zi   yuán
有的（桌子）圆。

TIP In sentences with "有……，有的……，有的……", the noun that appears after "有的" may be omitted if it was already mentioned earlier in the sentence. This sentence structure is useful to describe variations in the appearance of objects.

中文

zì
字有大小，有的大，有的小。

zì   zì
"中"字大，"文"字小。

Reduplication of adjectives

A ➡ A A 的

TIP In general, monosyllabic adjectives which describe the properties of things can be reduplicated as "AA". They must be followed by "的" to associate with the nouns they describe.

yuán zhuō zi
圆桌子

yuán   zhuō zi
圆的桌子

yuán yuán   zhuō zi
圆圆的桌子

yuán yuán   zhuō zi
三张圆圆的桌子

yuán yuán   zhuō zi
小明家有三张圆圆的桌子

Go200 **WANT TO LEARN MORE?**

Check out the Text > Sentence Pattern section in the Go200 CD.

Let's TALK

Find a partner and practice the following dialogues.

Find a partner and practice the following dialogues.

⭐ Task 1

Ⓐ : 小明，你看见我哥哥了吗？

Ⓑ : 你哥哥什么样儿？
yàngr

Ⓐ : 他和我一样瘦，一样高
yí yàng shòu   yí yàng gāo

Ⓑ : 你哥哥穿什么？

Ⓐ : 他和我一样穿白(white)衣服。
yí yàng   bái   yī fu

Ⓑ : 我高高的瘦瘦的。

⭐ Task 2   long sentence

Ⓐ : 什么是长句子？
cháng jù zi

Ⓑ : 有逗号(comma)的句子，是长句子。
dòu hào   jù zi   cháng jù zi

Ⓐ : 你会说长句子吗？
cháng jù zi

Ⓑ : 会！我会说长句子。"我哥哥高高的，
cháng jù zi   gāo gāo
胖胖的，他会说很多中文。"
pàng pàng

New Words

様儿 yàngr one's appearance; pattern

一样 yí yàng the same

The reduplicated adjectives in the sentence— "高高的" and "胖胖的"—serve to limit or differentiate.

 Task 3

(A conversation between a sales assistant and a customer.)

Ⓐ: 你好！请问你要买什么？

Ⓑ: 我要买一张桌子(zhuō zi)。

Ⓐ: 你要什么样儿(yàngr)的桌子(zhuō zi)？

Ⓑ: 我要圆桌子(yuán zhuō zi)。

Ⓐ: 你要大桌子(zhuō zi)，还是小桌子(zhuō zi)？
　　= or

Ⓑ: 我要大桌子(zhuō zi)。

Ⓐ: 请你等一等，我去找一张圆圆的大桌子(yuán yuán zhuō zi)。
　　= wait　　　　zhǎo =
　　　　　　　　　Look
　　　　　　　　　for

Ⓑ: 好，谢谢你！

TIP

A question with "还是" provides a choice. To answer, one simply chooses the answer before or after "还是".

 Task 4

Ⓐ: 那张桌子上(zhuō zi shàng)有什么？

Ⓑ: 桌子上 有两本书。

Ⓐ: 你看到(kàn dào)哥哥的书包了吗？

Ⓑ: Wo kan dao 哥哥书包在桌
　　　　　　　　　　　　　　　　　子下

The following dialogues are adapted from the dialogues in your (Go 200). You may listen to the CD before reading the transcript on this page.

★ Task 5

tat or not.

A: 你弟弟 胖 不 胖 (pàng pàng)?

B: 我弟弟不胖，他很瘦 (pàng shòu)。

A: 你姐姐 高 不 高 (gāo gāo)?

B: 我姐姐很高 (gāo)。你姐姐高吗 (gāo)?

A: 我姐姐不高也(also)不矮 (gāo yě ǎi)。

★ Task 6

kind of what.

A: 你要什么样儿的桌子 (yàngr zhuō zi)?

B: 我要方桌子 (fāng zhuō zi)。

A: 这里(here)有很多方桌子，你要哪一个 (zhè lǐ fāng zhuō zi)?

B: Wo de ai ai de fang zhuo zi.
我要矮矮的桌子

(Go 200)

WANT TO LEARN MORE?

Check out the Text > Dialogue section in the Go200 CD.

Let's Learn CHARACTER

 Sequence of Writing Chinese Characters

From Left to Right

Most Chinese characters are made up of two parts written side by side. When writing such characters, you should start with the component on the left before proceeding to the one on the right.

Structure of Chinese Characters

Thin Left Component and Wide Right Component

In many characters with two parts, the left and right components may or may not be in proportion to each other. For example, "他" has a narrow left component and a wide right component, while "对" is made up of two proportionate components.

yǐ

pàng

 **Trace It**

What is the first stroke for each of the characters below? Trace it out.

①  ②  ③

Text 1  Go 200

Read the following text carefully.

pàng zi　　　　shòu zi
大胖子*，小瘦子*。

pàng zi　　pàng　　　shòu zi　　shòu
胖子说胖好，瘦子说瘦好。

pàng zi　　　　shòu zi　　shòu　　　shòu zi　　　　pàng zi　　pàng
大胖子说小瘦子太瘦，小瘦子说大胖子太胖。

*胖子 the fat one

*瘦子 the thin one

Answer these questions in Chinese.

1　Who says it is good being fat? Who says it is good being thin?

2　"小贵太胖、小明不胖、大关有一点儿胖"—who is the fattest of them all?

3a) Can you state the differences between the three characters below?

b) Fill in the blanks below with "大" or "太" appropriately.

(1) 我的书包__大__，妹妹的书包小。

(2) 妹妹__太__小了，不可以去上学。

Twist Your Tongue

Read the text above as a tongue twister. Compete with a friend to see who can read it clearly and fluently.

Read the following text carefully.

我叫王大关，今年十三岁。我高高的，脸*
gāo gāo liǎn

yuán yuán pàng
圆圆的，有一点儿胖。

我有很多同学，有的同学胖胖的，有的同
pàng pàng
学瘦瘦的，有的同学高高的，有的同学矮矮的。
shòu shòu gāo gāo ǎi ǎi

我有很多同学，有的脸方方的，有的脸圆圆的，
liǎn fāng fāng liǎn yuán yuán
有的脸长长的。
liǎn cháng cháng

我有很多同学，大家都不一样*。
bù yí yàng

*脸 face

*不一样 different

Answer these questions in Chinese.

1 Can you describe the author's looks?
2 Why does the author say that everybody looks different?
3 How many students in your class are thin? How many are tall?

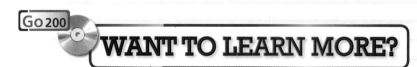

WANT TO LEARN MORE?

Check out the Text > Reading section in the Go200 CD.

Let's DO IT

Look at the four people below. Carry out the following conversation and state their similarities and differences.

Joe　　Paul　　Henry　　Mike

Ⓐ: Joe 和 Henry 哪里(which part)^{nǎ lǐ}一样^{yí yàng}？

Ⓑ: Joe 和 Henry 都戴白^{bái}帽子。

Ⓐ: Joe 和 Henry 哪里不一样^{nǎ lǐ bù yí yàng}？

Ⓑ: Joe 背书包，Henry 没背书包。

LEARNING LOG

I can...	Excellent 😃	Good 🙂	Fair 😐	Needs Improvement ☹️
1　describe objects with adjectives such as "大", "小", "圆", "方", "长", and "短".	☐	☐	☐	☐
2　describe people as "胖", "瘦", "高", or "矮".	☐	☐	☐	☐
3　describe the location of an object—whether it is above, below, or inside something else.	☐	☐	☐	☐
4　Use reduplication of adjectives in sentences appropriately.	☐	☐	☐	☐
5　write Chinese characters from left to right.	☐	☐	☐	☐
6　write "高", "方", "圆", "长", and "短".	☐	☐	☐	☐

多看多听
Look More & Listen More

My Goals

1 Name my sense organs and limbs in Chinese
2 State the uses of my sense organs and limbs
3 Use appropriate measure words to talk about my sense organs and limbs
4 Understand the principle of writing horizontal strokes before vertical strokes in Chinese
5 Become familiar with vocabulary associated with my sense organs and their functions

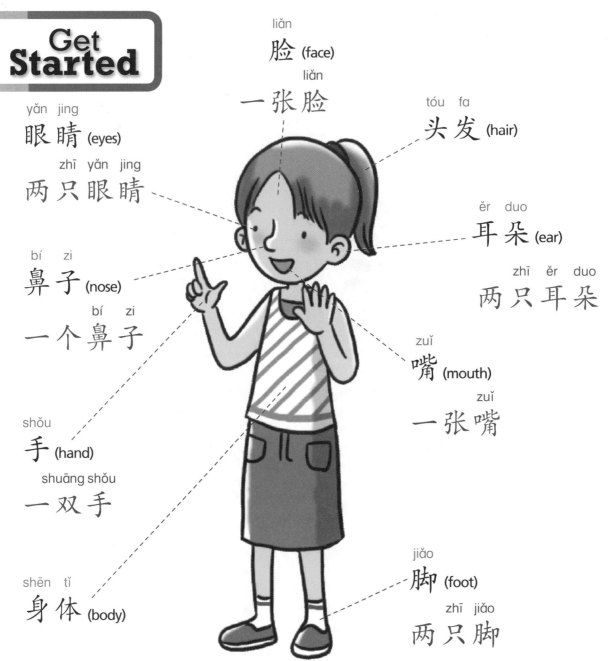

liǎn
脸 (face)

liǎn
一张脸

tóu fa
头发 (hair)

yǎn jing
眼睛 (eyes)

zhī yǎn jing
两只眼睛

ěr duo
耳朵 (ear)

zhī ěr duo
两只耳朵

bí zi
鼻子 (nose)

bí zi
一个鼻子

zuǐ
嘴 (mouth)

zuǐ
一张嘴

shǒu
手 (hand)

shuāng shǒu
一双手

jiǎo
脚 (foot)

zhī jiǎo
两只脚

shēn tǐ
身体 (body)

⭐ Play It

Take turns to recite a chant by naming body parts three times. Point to the body parts as you name them. Surprise your partner by changing the last body part in the chant. Your partner has to point to any other body part except the one you have just named.

bí zi bí zi
鼻子，鼻子

yǎn jing
眼睛

New Words

zhī
只 (a measure word used for one of a pair, or for certain animals)

shuāng
双 pair

Let's CHANT Go 200

zhī yǎn jing yī zhāng zuǐ
两只眼睛一张嘴，

zhī ěr duo shuāng shǒu
两只耳朵一双手，

duō kàn duō xué duō zuò shì
多看多学多做事，

duō tīng duō wèn bù huì wàng
多听多问不会忘。

TIP

How do you distinguish between "二", "两", and "双"?

➤ "二" is a number that can be used in counting and as an ordinal number.

➤ "两" is used before a measure word.

➤ "双" is a measure word for two of the same thing, for example, "一双手" (a pair of hands), "一双鞋" (a pair of shoes).

New Words

yǎn jing 眼睛 eyes	zuǐ 嘴 mouth	ěr duo 耳朵 ear	shǒu 手 hand
duō 多 more	zuò 做 do	zuò shì 做事 do something	tīng 听 listen	wàng 忘 forget

多看多听 39

Let's Learn GRAMMAR

我有	yǎn jing 眼睛，	我用	yǎn jing 眼睛	看。
	ěr duo 耳朵，		ěr duo 耳朵	tīng 听。

yǎn jing 眼睛	看	看书
ěr duo 耳朵	tīng 听	
zuǐ 嘴	问　说	问问题　说话(speak) shuō huà
shǒu 手		zuò shì 做事　打字 dǎ zì

yǎn jing 　　　　yǎn jing
我有眼睛，我用眼睛看书。

shǒu 　　　　shǒu dǎ zì
我有手，我用手打字。

zuǐ 　　　　zuǐ
我有嘴，我用嘴问问题。

New Words

dǎ zì
打字 type

WANT TO LEARN MORE?

Check out the Text > Sentence Pattern section in the Go200 CD.

是……的

这本书是弟弟的。

这台电脑是哥哥的。

The phrase following "的" has been omitted here. The original sentence should read "这台电脑是哥哥的电脑。".

我的帽子是白 (white) 的，他的帽子也 (also) 是白的。

bái　　　　　　　yě　　bái

"两只手" 和 "一双手"
zhī shǒu　　　　shuāng shǒu

是一样的。

TIP

"是……的" is used to clarify or describe something, with the intention to emphasize.
"我的书包是妈妈买的。" clarifies that it was Mother who bought the bag and not someone else.

我的书包是妈妈买的。

duō
多

老师说："我们要多看、多学、
duō　　　duō
多做事。"
duō zuò shì

妈妈说："我们要多学中文、
duō
多用电脑、多看书。"
duō　　　duō

爸爸说："我们要多用眼睛、
duō　　yǎn jing
多用耳朵、多用手。"
duō　ěr duo　duō shǒu

TIP

When used as an adverb, "多" means "more". In Chinese, the adverb "多" is placed before the verb whereas in English, the adverb "more" is placed after the verb.

"多" is also often used with "一点儿", for example, "多吃一点儿"(eat more), "多做一点儿"(do more), "多看一点儿"(look around more).

Find a partner and practice the following dialogues.

Task 1

Ⓐ：哥哥，你在做^{zuò}什么？

Ⓑ：我在做^{zuò}椅子，我用手做^{shǒu zuò}椅子。

Ⓐ：爸爸，你在做^{zuò}什么？

Ⓒ：我在做^{zuò}桌子，我用手做^{shǒu zuò}桌子。

Task 2 forget

Ⓐ：我忘^{wàng}了今天是星期几了。

Ⓑ：今天是星期四。

Ⓐ：我忘^{wàng}了星期四我要做^{zuò}什么了。

Ⓑ：星期四你要和同学去买书。

Ⓐ：我忘^{wàng}了几点要去买书了。

Task 3

妹妹：妈妈，我有两只手。
zhī shǒu

妈妈：对，你有两只手。
zhī shǒu

姐姐：妈妈，我有一双手。
shuāng shǒu

妈妈：对，你有一双手。
shuāng shǒu

两只手和一双手是一样的。
zhī shǒu shuāng shǒu

the same

Task 4

What can you do with your sense organs? Discuss this with your partner and then carry out the following conversation.

Ⓐ: 你的眼睛可以做什么？
yǎn jing zuò

Ⓑ: 我用眼睛看 _____

Ⓐ: 你的嘴可以做什么？
zuǐ zuò

Ⓑ: 我用嘴说话 _____ 。

Ⓐ: 你的耳朵可以做什么？
ěr duo zuò

Ⓑ: 我用耳朵听 _____ 。

Ⓐ: 你的手可以做什么？
shǒu zuò

Ⓑ: 我用手做事 _____ 。 （可以……，还可以……）

In the eight sentences below, can you identify pairs of sentences which make up a conversation? Group the following sentences into four sets of conversation and record them in the table below. When you are done, you may listen to the conversations in the CD for the right answers.

①	A: 3	②	A: 1	③	A: 7	④	A: 4
	B: 2		B: 76		B: 5		B: 8

❶ 小明！小明！

❷ 对不起，我忘了。Sorry I forgot
   wàng

❸ 你忘了吗？今天是我的生日 (birthday)。
   wàng   *shēng rì*

❹ 你有没有打电话？

❺ 我在打字。typing
   dǎ zi

❻ 什么事？你叫我有什么事？
   shì   *shì*

❼ 你在做什么？
   zuò

❽ 我还没（有）打。

Go 200

WANT TO LEARN MORE?

Check out the Text > Dialogue section in the Go200 CD.

Let's Learn
CHARACTER

⭐ Sequence of Writing Chinese Characters

Horizontal Strokes before Vertical Strokes

When there is a criss-crossing of horizontal and vertical strokes in a Chinese character, you should first write the horizontal stroke before writing the vertical one. When a character is made up of many horizontal strokes and one vertical stroke with a hook, you should write all the horizontal strokes before finally writing the vertical stroke with the hook.

shǒu shì

⭐ Structure of Chinese Characters

Placing the Left Component " 口 " Higher

A number of Chinese characters have " 口 " ("mouth" side) as the left component. In such characters, " 口 " is written slightly higher on the left. It also should not be written too big; it should only occupy a third of the width of the entire character.

tīng zuǐ

Let's READ

Text 1 Go 200

Read the following text carefully.

zhāng kāi yǎn　　　　　　　duō
张开*眼，我们可以多看，

ěr duo　　　　　　　duō tīng
有耳朵，我们可以多听，

zhāng kāi zuǐ　　　　　　　duō
张开嘴，我们可以多问。

dǎ kāi
打开*一本书，

我们可以看，我们可以学。

dǎ kāi
打开电脑，我们可以看，可以学，

tīng　　　　　　　dǎ zì
可以听，还可以打字。

*张开 open
*打开 open with hands

TIP
If you require your hands to "open" something, you
　　　　　　　　dǎ kāi
should use the verb "打开".

Answer these questions in Chinese.

1　Which of our sense organs do we see with? Hear with? Ask questions with?
2　What are the uses of computers?
3　Is "张" in "张开嘴" the same as "张" in "一张纸"? Do you know how they are used respectively?

 46　多看多听

Read the following text carefully.

妹妹的眼睛大大的，我的眼睛小小的。哥哥的手大大的，我的手小小的。弟弟的嘴大大的，我的嘴小小的。

妈妈说："我们有一双手，我们要多用手做事。我们有两只眼睛，我们要多用眼睛看书。我们有一张嘴，我们要多用嘴问问题。多看、多做、多问问题可以学会很多事。"

Answer these questions in Chinese.

1 Are the author's eyes big? What about his hands? What about his mouth?
2 Why should we look around us more, use our hands more, and ask more questions?
3 Which part of our body do we use to do things? To read a book? To ask questions?

WANT TO LEARN MORE?

Check out the Text > Reading section in the Go200 CD.

Let's DO IT

Play this game in pairs or small teams. Use two coins as place markers. Take turns to toss another coin to move. One side of the coin lets you move one space; the other side lets you move two. If you land on a box with a phrase, your opponent will ask you to fit the phrase into either one of the sentence structures below. Give the right answer and stay put in the box. If you are wrong, go back to the nearest blank box.

① (手_{shǒu}) 可以做_{zuò}什么？
(手_{shǒu}) 可以 (做事_{zuò shì})。

② 我有 (手_{shǒu})，
我用 (手_{shǒu}) (做事_{zuò shì})。

Start	1	2 看书	3 听 (tīng)
7 问问题	6 穿鞋子	5	4 做桌子 (zuò)
8 说中文	9	10 戴眼镜 (yǎn jìng) (wear glasses)	11 说话 (shuō huà) (speak)
End	14 回答问题	13 打字 (dǎ zì)	12

I can...

Excellent | Good | Fair | Needs Improvement

1 name my sense organs and my limbs.

2 describe my sense organs and count my limbs using the appropriate measure words.

3 state the uses of my sense organs and limbs.

4 clarify or describe something using "是……的".

5 write horizontal strokes before vertical ones when writing Chinese characters.

6 write "眼", "耳", "手", "听", and "做".

LEARNING LOG

LESSON 5

我吃什么?
What Do I Eat?

My Goals

1 Name some common food items in Chinese
2 Use "吃" and "喝" respectively on appropriate food and drinks
3 Be able to ask for and about various food items
4 Express the fact that an action has been completed
5 Understand how some Chinese characters evolved from illustrations
6 Become familiar with vocabulary associated with food

49

niú nǎi 牛奶 (milk)	guǒ zhī 果汁 (juice)	kā fēi 咖啡 (coffee)	chá 茶 (tea)	miàn bāo 面包 (bread)
sān míng zhì 三明治 (sandwich)	fàn 饭 (rice)	cài 菜 (course of a meal)	miàn 面 (noodles)	bāo zi 包子 (steamed bun with stuffing)

 **Play It**

Pair up with a partner and take turns to assign a food item to each other (you can select any food item of your choice). The person assigned with the food item must then state the appropriate verb to be used with it, as well as imitate the consumption of it.

New Words

hē
喝 drink

chī
吃 eat

Let's
CHANT Go 200

zǎo shang niú nǎi hé miàn bāo
早上牛奶和面包，

zhong wu guǒ zhī sān míng zhì
中午果汁三明治，

wang? Y fàn yě cài
zhong shang
晚上有饭也有菜，

chī bǎo hē gòu Shuo xiè xiè
吃饱喝够说谢谢。

New Words

zǎo shang 早上 morning	niú nǎi 牛奶 milk	miàn bāo 面包 bread	guǒ zhī 果汁 juice	sān míng zhì 三明治 sandwich
yě 也 also	fàn 饭 rice; meal	cài 菜 course (of a meal); vegetable	chī bǎo 吃饱 eat till one is full	gòu 够 enough

Let's Learn GRAMMAR

你 要 吃(chī) 面包(miàn bāo) 吗？

你要喝牛奶吗？(hē niú nǎi)

你 吃不吃(chī chī) 饭(fàn)？

你喝不喝牛奶？(hē hē niú nǎi)

⭐ Want More Practice?

Fit the following words into the sentence structures on this page to form new sentences.

三明治(sān míng zhì)　包子(bāo zi)　果汁(guǒ zhī)

菜(cài)　　面(miàn)

要……，还要…… / 要……，也要……(yě)

我要吃面包，还要喝牛奶。(chī miàn bāo hē niú nǎi)

我要吃面包，也要喝牛奶。(chī miàn bāo yě hē niú nǎi)

我不要吃面包。我不要喝牛奶。(chī miàn bāo hē niú nǎi)

我不要吃面包，也不要喝牛奶。(chī miàn bāo yě hē niú nǎi)

TIP "还" indicates an addition to what was expressed before it. The additional matter is indicated after "还".

"也" between two phrases is more neutral, indicating that the actions in both phrases are mutually consistent.

我什么都不要。

TIP When you do not wish to take up any offer from another person, you may say "我什么都不要。".

了

zǎo shang　chī　sān míng zhì
早上我吃了三明治。

zǎo shang　hē　guǒ zhī
早上我喝了果汁。

chī　fàn
中午我吃了饭。
中午我看了书。

New Words

zǎo fàn
早饭 breakfast

bēi
杯 a cup of (a measure word used for drinks)

hē　guǒ zhī　chī　sān míng zhì
我喝了果汁，还吃了三明治。

zǎo shang　chī　zǎo fàn
星期六早上，我吃了早饭，还看了书。

哥哥学了三年中文了。

hē　bēi niú nǎi
我喝了两杯牛奶了。

TIP

"了" can mean the completion of an action, or it can mean a change in the state. On this page, all occurrences of "了" after a verb indicate the end of an action. In "哥哥学了三年中文了。", the first "了" indicates that the act of learning (学) has been completed; the second "了" at the end of the sentence expresses a state that has been changed at this point in time.

Go 200

WANT TO LEARN MORE?

Check out the Text > Sentence Pattern section in the Go200 CD.

Find a partner and practice the following dialogues.

★ Task 1

A: 我要<u>买</u>一个三明治，<u>还要</u>一杯果汁。
mǎi　sān míng zhì　hái yào　　bēi guǒ zhī

B: 好。还要什么吗？要不要牛奶？
niú nǎi

A: 不要了，请问<u>一共</u>多少钱？
yí gòng　in total

B: 一共五块钱。

★ Task 2

A: 你早上<u>喝不喝</u>牛奶？
zǎo shang hē　hē niú nǎi

B: 我早上不喝牛奶。
zǎo shang　hē niú nǎi

A: 你早上<u>吃不吃</u>三明治？
zǎo shang chī　chī sān míng zhì

B: 我早上也不吃三明治。早上我吃饭和菜。
zǎo shang yě　chī sān míng zhì　zǎo shang　chī fàn　cài

A: 吃了早饭，你做什么？
chī　zǎo fàn

B: 吃<u>饱</u>了，我和弟弟一起<u>去上学</u>。
chī bǎo

Task 3

(At home)

妈妈： 你要<ruby>吃<rt>chī</rt></ruby><ruby>面包<rt>miàn bāo</rt></ruby>吗？

大关： 我要<ruby>吃<rt>chī</rt></ruby><ruby>面包<rt>miàn bāo</rt></ruby>。

妈妈： 你要<ruby>喝<rt>hē</rt></ruby><ruby>果汁<rt>guǒ zhī</rt></ruby>吗？

大关： 我要<ruby>喝<rt>hē</rt></ruby><ruby>果汁<rt>guǒ zhī</rt></ruby>。

我要<ruby>吃<rt>chī</rt></ruby><ruby>面包<rt>miàn bāo</rt></ruby>，<ruby>也<rt>yě</rt></ruby>要<ruby>喝<rt>hē</rt></ruby><ruby>果汁<rt>guǒ zhī</rt></ruby>。

(In school)

老师： <ruby>早上<rt>zǎo shang</rt></ruby>你<ruby>吃<rt>chī</rt></ruby>了什么？

大关： 我<ruby>吃<rt>chī</rt></ruby>了<ruby>面包<rt>miàn bāo</rt></ruby>，还<ruby>喝<rt>hē</rt></ruby>了<ruby>果汁<rt>guǒ zhī</rt></ruby>。

老师： <ruby>面包<rt>miàn bāo</rt></ruby>好<ruby>吃<rt>chī</rt></ruby>吗？

大关： <ruby>面包<rt>miàn bāo</rt></ruby>很好<ruby>吃<rt>chī</rt></ruby>。

老师： <ruby>果汁<rt>guǒ zhī</rt></ruby>好<ruby>喝<rt>hē</rt></ruby>吗？

大关： <ruby>果汁<rt>guǒ zhī</rt></ruby>很好<ruby>喝<rt>hē</rt></ruby>。

★ Task 4

Ⓐ : 你们好！你们要吃什么，喝什么？
  chī　　　hē

Ⓑ : 我要一个三明治。
  sān míng zhì

Ⓒ : 我要一杯果汁。
  bēi guǒ zhī

Ⓓ : 我什么都不要。

Ⓐ : 一个三明治和一杯果汁，
  sān míng zhì　　bēi guǒ zhī

　　一共七块三。谢谢！

★ Task 5

The following dialogue can be found in your  Go 200 . You may listen to the CD before reading the transcript.

Ⓐ : 吃饱了吗？多吃
  chī bǎo　　chī
　　一点儿。

Ⓑ : 够了！够了！我
  gòu　　gòu
　　吃饱了！谢谢！
  chī bǎo

enough

> **TIP** Eating is an important part of the Chinese culture. When entertaining guests, Chinese hosts often worry that their guests will go hungry. Hence, the host will often ask his guest to "多吃一点儿。" (eat more).
>
> "你吃饱了吗？" (Have you eaten?) is also a common greeting between the Chinese when they meet. In reply to such a greeting, it is fine to simply give a straightforward answer of either "yes" or "not yet"; there is no need for further elaboration.

> "了" in the phrase "够了" is a modal particle. It shows the occurrence and continuation of a state ("够" in this case).

Let's Learn CHARACTER

★ The Origin of Chinese Characters

Many Chinese characters evolved from illustrations. Look at the examples below. Can you tell what character each of the following illustrations has evolved into? Write it down.

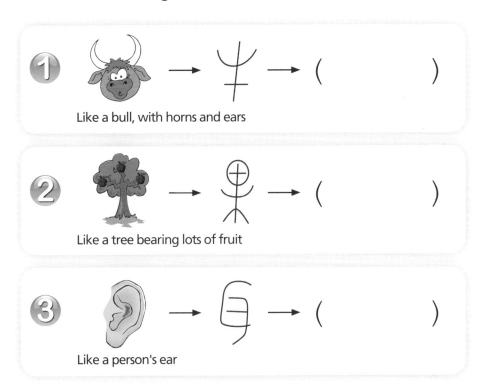

1 Like a bull, with horns and ears → ( )

2 Like a tree bearing lots of fruit → ( )

3 Like a person's ear → ( )

★ Alternative Way to Remember Chinese Characters

"Break Down" Characters

An alternative way to remember Chinese characters is to "break down" a character to explain it.

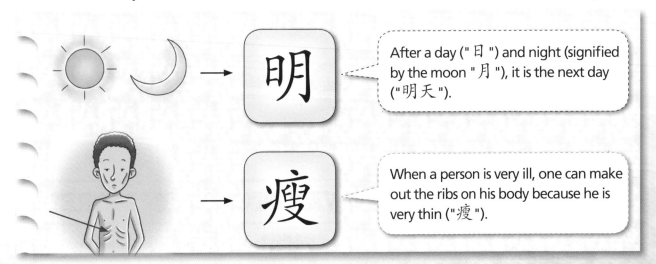

After a day ("日") and night (signified by the moon "月"), it is the next day ("明天").

When a person is very ill, one can make out the ribs on his body because he is very thin ("瘦").

Read the following text carefully.

guǒ zhī   hē   hē
果汁很好喝，不要多喝。

fàn cài   chī   chī
饭菜很好吃，不要多吃。

电脑很有用，我们要学。

                              yě
中文很有用，我们也要学。

Answer these questions in Chinese.

1 What food items were mentioned in the passage above? Of the above food items, which one do you consume by eating, and which one do you consume by drinking? Categorize them in the table below.

chī
吃   fan 饭菜 cai

hē
喝   果汁 ✓

2 What did the author say not to eat too much of, what not to drink too much of, and what to learn more of? zhong when hen you yong

3 In what way is the computer useful to us? In what way is learning Chinese useful?

You can reasearch:
wo men be yi da
zi
可以 打字

You 可以 说中文 ✓

Check out the Text > Reading section in the Go200 CD.

Text 2

Read the following text carefully.

今天早上我和妈妈去买早饭。我们买了果汁、牛奶、三明治，还买了面包。

我吃了一个三明治，妹妹也吃了一个三明治。我喝了一杯牛奶，妹妹也喝了一杯牛奶。爸爸吃了两个面包，还喝了两杯牛奶。妈妈不吃三明治，也不喝牛奶。妈妈喝了两杯果汁。

我天天*和家人一起吃早饭。

*天天 every day

Answer these questions in Chinese.

1　What did the author buy?

sān míng zhì	miàn bāo	guǒ zhī	niú nǎi
三明治	面包	果汁	牛奶
两个	两个	两杯	四杯

他买了两个三明治、两个面包，两棵汁
和四杯牛奶。

2　Who had sandwiches and milk for breakfast? Who had bread for breakfast?
3　What did the author's mother have for breakfast? 两杯果汁

我吃什么？　59

Let's DO IT

1 Using the following sentences, ask your group members what they had for breakfast. On a piece of paper, draw the table below and fill it in.

Ⓐ： 请问你早饭吃了什么？喝了什么？
zǎo fàn chī   hē

Ⓑ： 今天早上我吃了_____，还喝了_____。
zǎo shang chī   hē

姓名	面包 miàn bāo	三明治 sān míng zhì	牛奶 niú nǎi	果汁 guǒ zhī	咖啡 kā fēi	Others
1 Adam	V			V		
2						

2 Do a tally of all the food that your group had for breakfast. One member from each group will then present the survey to the class.

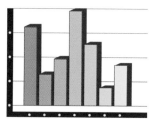

3 Individual assignment — plot a graph on a piece of paper with the survey data of all the groups.

LEARNING LOG

I can...

		Excellent	Good	Fair	Needs Improvement
1	say some common food items such as milk, bread, juice, and sandwich in Chinese.	☐	☐	☐	☐
2	use "吃" and "喝" respectively on appropriate food and drinks.	☐	☐	☐	☐
3	use "了" to indicate that I have finished an action.	☐	☐	☐	☐
4	use "吃不吃?" and "喝不喝?" to ask what others might like to eat or drink.	☐	☐	☐	☐
5	explain how "牛", "果", and "耳" have evolved from illustrations.	☐	☐	☐	☐
6	write "牛", "果", "吃", "喝", and "饭".	☐	☐	☐	☐

走路开车
Walking &
Driving

My Goals

1 State what the colors of traffic lights mean, and remind others of road safety
2 Use prepositions of location to indicate the position of objects
3 Use reduplication of some verbs and prepositions of location in my expressions
4 Understand the principle of writing the bottom stroke last when writing fully framed Chinese characters
5 Become familiar with vocabulary associated with walking and driving on the road

chē
车
(vehicle)

kāi chē
开车
(drive)

zǒu lù
走路
(walk)

hóng lǜ dēng
红绿灯
(traffic lights)

hóng dēng
红灯
(red light)

lǜ dēng
绿灯
(green light)

hòu miàn
后面

qián miàn
前面

shàng miàn
上面

xià miàn
下面

zuǒ biān
左边

yòu biān
右边

Describe It

Look at the picture on page 61. Describe what you see in the picture, and use "在 + preposition of location" to describe the positions of the items in relation to one another. For example, "红灯在绿灯上面。".

New Words

shàng miàn 上面 on top; above	xià miàn 下面 under
zuǒ biān 左边 left side	yòu biān 右边 right side
qián miàn 前面 front	hòu miàn 后面 behind; back

Let's CHANT Go 200

zǒu lù kāi chē yào xiǎo xīn
走路开车要小心，

zuǒ kàn kan yòu kàn kan
左看看，右看看，

kàn hóng dēng jiù tíng
看见红灯我就停，

lǜ dēng
看见绿灯可以走。

TIP Traffic lights may appear differently in different countries, but red always means "stop" and green means "go". Besides red and green, other colors are sometimes used for pedestrian signals in some countries. For example, in some cities in the United States, a white signal tells pedestrians that they can cross the street.

New Words

zǒu lù 走路 walk	kāi chē 开车 drive	xiǎo xīn 小心 be careful	zuǒ 左 left	yòu 右 right
hóng dēng 红灯 red light	jiù 就 just	tíng 停 stop	lǜ dēng 绿灯 green light	

Let's Learn GRAMMAR

（一）看见红灯， 我 就 停。
hóng dēng *jiù* *tíng*

（一）看见小明，我就叫他。
jiù

早上（一）看见老师，
弟弟就说老师早。
jiù

姐姐（一）回家 (back home)，
huí jiā
就打电话。
jiù

妹妹（一）看见妈妈，就不哭 (cry) 了。
jiù *kū*

TIP

Sentences with "一……，就……" can mean that the actions in the sentence occur consecutively, or that one is a condition of the other. When the emphasis is on the verb after "就"， "一" in front may be omitted.

The subject of the sentence may be placed in either the first clause or the second, for example, "我一看见红灯，就停。"，or "一看见红灯，我就停。".

就是……
jiù shì

我就是Tom。
jiù shì

他就是王老师。
jiù shì

这就是弟弟的书包。
jiù shì

九点半就是九点三十分。
jiù shì

TIP

"我是Tom。" and "我就是Tom。" mean the same. "就是……" is used to reinforce the tone of the expression.

New Words

就是 am or is (with added emphasis)
jiù shì

Reduplication of Verbs

A ➜ A 一 A
A ➜ A A

走 ➜ 走一走 / 走走

听 ➜ 听一听 / 听听 *zhǎo = look for (V V)*

找 ➜ 找一找 / 找找

看 ➜ 看一看 / 看看

TIP
Verbs describing action may be reduplicated in the following ways:
➤ V ➜ V 一 V
➤ V ➜ V V
Here, reduplication can mean "to have a go at something" (e.g. 看一看 = have a look), or brief actions that are performed repetitively (e.g. 看看 = looking around).

Reduplication of Prepositions of Location

AB ➜ AABB

上下 ➜ 上上下下

我的书不见了，我上上下下都没看见。

zuǒ yòu　　　 zuǒ zuǒ yòu yòu
左右 ➜ 左左右右

zuǒ zuǒ yòu yòu
左左右右都是人，很多人。

TIP
Reduplicating these prepositions of location indicates an extensive and complete coverage of a particular space. For example, "上上下下都没看见" means to search high and low, not leaving any stone unturned.

qián hòu　　 qián qián hòu hòu
前后 ➜ 前前后后

qián qián hòu hòu　　　　 chē　　 kāi chē　　 xiǎo xīn
前前后后都是车，开车要小心。

Go 200

WANT TO LEARN MORE?

Check out the Text > Sentence Pattern section in the Go200 CD.

Find a partner and practice the following dialogues.

Task 1

hěn duō = a lot

A: 小明，你爸爸会开车吗？
kāi chē

B: 我爸爸不会开车，你爸爸会开车吗？
kāi chē kāi chē

A: 他会开车，他开车去上班(go to work)。
kāi chē kāi chē shàng bān

B: 我爸爸不会开车，他走路去上班。
kāi chē zǒu lù shàng bān

> **TIP**
>
> In different countries, people drive and walk on different sides of the road. In China, people drive and walk on the _right_ side of the road; pedestrians must first check for cars on their left before crossing the road safely. In other countries like England, people drive and walk on the _left_ side of the road. Pedestrains crossing the road must then look out for cars on their right first before crossing.

Task 2

妈妈，我吃饱了，我要去上学了。

路上有很多车，走路要小心。
lù chē zǒu lù xiǎo xīn

要左看看，右看看，小心车子。
zǒu yòu xiǎo xīn chē zi

我会小心的。看到红灯我就停，看到绿灯
xiǎo xīn hóng dēng jiù tíng lù dēng

可以走。

> Here, "的" serves as an emphasis or affirmation.

⭐Task 3

Ⓐ : 你好，我找谢小明。✓   ✓

Ⓑ : 我就是谢小明。请问你是谁？
    jiù shì

Ⓐ : 我是王大关。明天就是我的生日 (birthday)，
    jiù shì shēng rì

    明天下午四点钟，你可以来我家吗？

Ⓑ : 可以。

⭐Task 4

Jay has just attained his driving license and is driving Tom, his younger brother, around in a car. Get a partner to pretend to be either Jay or Tom, and practice the following dialogue.

Tom : 哥哥，小心！前面有大车子！
      xiǎo xīn qián miàn chē zi

Tom : 哥哥，小心！左边有车子！
      xiǎo xīn zuǒ biān chē zi

Jay : 我看见了，我会小心的。
      xiǎo xīn

Tom : 哥哥，前前后后有很多车，你开车要小心。
      qián qián hòu hòu chē kāi chē xiǎo xīn

大车在前，
chē qián
小车在后。
chē hòu

红车在左，
hóng chē zuǒ
绿车在右。
lù chē yòu

Task 5 [Go 200]

1 Organize the following eight utterances into three dialogues and fill in the table below. When this is done, you may listen to the dialogues in the CD for the right answers.

① A:		② A:		③ A:
B:		B:		B:
A:				
B:				

huí jiā
❶ 爸爸回家了吗？

lù chē zi   zǒu lù xiǎo xīn
❷ 路上车子多，走路小心一点儿。

❸ 你要大的还是小的？

bái   hóng
白 (white)的还是红(red)的？

> Here, the specific items after "的" have been omitted. For instance:
>
> A: 你要哪一本本子？
> B: 我要红的（本子）。
>
> A: 你要哪一个面包？
> B: 我要大的（面包）。

kāi chē   zǒu lù
❹ 我们开车去？还是走路去？

xiǎo xīn
❺ 谢谢。我会小心的。

huí jiā
❻ 爸爸还没（有）回家。

zǒu lù
❼ 我们走路去。

hóng
❽ 我要那个小的，红的。谢谢！

2 Expand dialogues 2 and 3 to four utterances per dialogue.

[Go 200]

WANT TO LEARN MORE?

Check out the Text > Dialogue section in the Go200 CD.

Sequence of Writing Chinese Characters

Fully Framed Characters: Bottom Stroke Last

For characters which have closed frames (e.g. "回", "面"), you should write the outer frame first, leaving the bottom open to fill in the inner strokes before closing the outer frame with the final stroke at the bottom.

Structure of Chinese Characters

Partially Framed Characters

Some Chinese characters have a partial frame on the left, so it looks like the right component is under the left component. When writing such characters, you should write the outer strokes before the inner strokes.

zuǒ

yòu

Let's READ

Read the following text carefully.

我的帽子不见了！

qián qián hòu hòu
前前后后，找一找，

上上下下，找一找，

zuǒ zuǒ yòu yòu
左左右右，找一找，

方桌子上，圆椅子下，

都没有看见我的帽子。

Answer these questions in Chinese.

1 Why was the author looking for his hat?
2 Where did the author search for his hat?
3 Did the author eventually find his hat?
4 Which of the following locations do you think the author will most possibly find his hat?
   Put a tick in the box next to the picture.

Text 2

Read the following text carefully.

kāi chē　　　zǒu lù
你开车，我走路。你要买菜，我要上学。

kāi chē　　xiǎo xīn　　　　zǒu lù　　　　xiǎo xīn
你开车要小心，我走路也要小心。

dǎ kāi　　　　　dǎ kāi
你打开*书，我打开电脑。

你要看书，我要打字。

dǎ kāi dēng
晚上你打开灯*看书。

dǎ kāi dēng
晚上我也要打开灯打字。

kāi xīn　　　　kāi xīn　　　　　kāi xīn
你开心*，我开心。我们都开心。

* 打开 open, switch on

* 灯 lamp

* 开心 happy

Answer these questions in Chinese.

1　How does the author go to school?　开车

2　Why is there a need to switch on the light? What does the author do with the light switched on?

3　Translate the following into English:

(i) 开车　　(ii) 打开电脑　　(iii) 打开灯

(iv) 打开书　　(v) 开心

WANT TO LEARN MORE?

Check out the Text > Reading section in the Go200 CD.

Let's DO IT

1 Get into a group of three — one to do the action, one to give the command, and one to be the judge. Rotate the roles during the game.

2 Each group will prepare the following items:

杯子　白纸　书　笔　书包　帽子

3 (i) The student doing the action will ask:

什么在前？　什么在后？　什么在左？　什么在右？
什么在上？　什么在下？

(ii) The student giving the command will say:

书包在前，杯子在后，帽子在左，书在右，
白纸在上，笔在下。

(The words in red may be used interchangeably by this student.)

(iii) From the perspective of the student doing the action, he has to place the items according to the instructions he was given. The judge will decide if he has done it correctly or incorrectly.

4 If time permits, groups can compete against one another.

LEARNING LOG

I can...	Excellent	Good	Fair	Needs Improvement
1 use vocabulary such as "走", "停", and "小心" to warn others of road safety.	☐	☐	☐	☐
2 use prepositions of location such as "上面", "下面", "左边", "右边", "前面", and "后面" to indicate the position of an object.	☐	☐	☐	☐
3 use reduplication of verbs and prepositions of location in my sentences appropriately.	☐	☐	☐	☐
4 recall that I should save the last stroke for the outer frame in fully framed characters.	☐	☐	☐	☐
5 write "路", "心", "车", "灯", and "红".	☐	☐	☐	☐

我玩游戏
Playing Games

My Goals

1. Identify five common colors in Chinese and use them to describe objects
2. Describe the activities in a particular place
3. Ask others if they would like to engage in a certain activity
4. Use Chinese punctuation " ？ " and " ！ " appropriately
5. Become familiar with vocabulary associated with colors and day-to-day activities

bái   sè
白 色

bái   yún
白 云 (white cloud)

bái
白 鞋 (white shoes)

hēi   sè
黑 色

hēi
黑 笔 (black pen)

hēi
黑 帽 子 (black cap)

lán   sè
蓝 色

lán   tiān
蓝 天 (blue sky)

lán
蓝 帽 子 (blue hat)

hóng   sè
红 色

红 灯

hóng
红 鞋 (red shoes)

lù   sè
绿 色

lù   cǎo   dì
绿 草 地 (green meadow or lawn)

绿 灯

New Words

bái   sè
白 色 white

hēi   sè
黑 色 black

lán   sè
蓝 色 blue

hóng   sè
红 色 red

lù   sè
绿 色 green

⭐ Describe It

Observe the picture on page 73.
Describe what you see using the colors
white, black, blue, red, and green.

Let's CHANT  Go200

tiān lán lán　　lán lán tiān
天蓝蓝，蓝蓝天，

lán tiān bái yún　　tiān qì
蓝天白云好天气。

dǎ dǎ qiú　　sàn sàn bù
打打球，散散步，

lǜ cǎo dì　　wán yóu xì
绿草地上玩游戏。

TIP Reduplication of adjectives is used to intensify the degree of the adjective, give a more vivid description of the subject matter, as well as create a more colorful piece of writing. At the same time, the meaning of the original phrase is retained.

Read the chant again, do you sense the the vividness of the description?

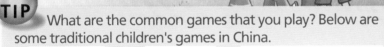

TIP What are the common games that you play? Below are some traditional children's games in China.

tī jiàn zi
踢毽子
kicking shuttlecock

dǎ tuó luó
打陀螺
spinning the top

dǒu kōng zhú
抖空竹
playing diabolo

On page 73, can you find the children playing these games?

New Words

lán tiān 蓝天 blue sky	bái yún 白云 white cloud	dǎ qiú 打球 play ball	tiān qì 天气 weather
sàn bù 散步 stroll	lǜ cǎo dì 绿草地 green meadow or lawn	wán 玩 play	yóu xì 游戏 games

Let's Learn GRAMMAR

Reduplication of Verbs
AB ➙ AAB

dǎ qiú
打球

dǎ qiú
一起去打球

cǎo dì　　dǎ qiú
一起去草地上打球

dǎ dǎ qiú
打打球

together

dǎ dǎ qiú
一起去打打球

cǎo dì　　dǎ dǎ qiú
一起去草地上打打球

看看书

玩 玩电脑游子戏

TIP

Reduplication of verbs may suggest that the action frequently takes place, or that there's no fixed time for the action to take place. Generally, reduplication of verbs creates a lighter tone. However, note that reduplication cannot be done on a verb describing an action that is presently taking place. For example:

✔ 我正在看书。　　✘ 我正在看看书。

★ **Want More Practice?**

Reduplicate and expand the following phrases in the same format as the examples on the left.

看书　　sàn bù
　　　　散步

wán　　yóu xì
玩电脑游戏

好不好?

We are together to play ball game　　yes or no / is it ok?

dǎ qiú
我们一起去打球，好不好?

On saturday come to my home　is it okay?
星期六来我家，好不好?

我们一起去上学，好不好?

We are together to go to school is
is okay?

TIP

To draw attention to the subject matter of a sentence, one can also place the question tag "好不好?" at the end of the sentence. In this case, "好不好?" serves to seek the opinion of the listener on the subject matter.

哥哥 people	在 at	草地上 test location	打球。 action
		家里	吃饭。

妈妈在家里吃早饭。爸爸在家里看书。

zài jiā lǐ

wán   yóu xì
弟弟在家里玩电脑游戏。
at home

cǎo dì
姐姐在草地上看书。
meadow/grassfeld

cǎo dì   sàn bù
爸爸和妈妈在草地上散步。

cǎo dì   dǎ qiú
哥哥和我在草地上打球。

TIP

In Chinese, one usually states the location before the action. This is different from English, where the adverbial phrase bearing the location is commonly placed at the end of a sentence. For example:

Chinese: 哥哥在草地上打球。
              location   action

English: My Brother plays ball on the lawn.
                        action   location

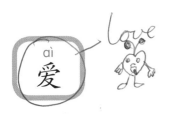

ài
爱
love

ài sàn bù
爸爸爱散步。

ài dǎ qiú
姐姐爱打球。

ài
哥哥爱看书。

ài
我爱学中文。

New Words

ài
爱 love

WANT TO LEARN MORE?

Check out the Text > Sentence Pattern section in the Go200 CD.

Find a partner and practice the following dialogues.

Task 1

A: 今天天气好吗？

B: 今天天气很好，有蓝天，有白云。

A: 今天天气很好，我们可以散散步，可以
打打球，也可以在草地上看看书。

Task 2

A: 明天你要做什么？

B: 天气好，我和弟弟在草地上
打球。天气不好，我和弟弟
在家里玩电脑游戏。

A: 明天我和你们一起玩，好不好？

B: 好。

Task 3

hòu tiān
后天是星期日，你要做什么？

péng you
我要和朋友 (friend) 一起吃饭。

hòu tiān   lái
后天你来我家，好不好？

好！

我们可以一起吃饭，

wán yóu xì
一起玩游戏。

谢谢你！

hòu tiān
后天我会去你家。

cafeteria

New Words

| 前天 | 昨天 | 今天 | 明天 | 后天 |

qián tiān
前天 the day before yesterday

hòu tiān
后天 the day after tomorrow

The following dialogues can be found in your [Go 200]. You may listen to the CD before reading the transcript on this page.

⭐Task 4

Ⓐ: 明天天气好吗？
　　　 tiān qì

Ⓑ: 明天天气很好，我们可以去散步。
　　　 tiān qì hen hao   ke yi qi sàn bù

⭐Task 5

Ⓐ: 明天去打球，好不好？
　　　　 dǎ qiú

Ⓑ: 对不起，明天我有事 (have something to do)，
　　 Dui baxi　　　　 yǒu shì

　　后天好不好？
　　 hòu tiān

⭐Task 6

Ⓐ: 这个星期六，
　　你要去哪里 (where) 玩？
　　　　　　 nǎ lǐ　 wán

Ⓑ: 这个星期六，我要去小明家玩。
　　　　　　　　　　　　　 wán

[Go 200]

WANT TO LEARN MORE?

Check out the Text > Dialogue section in the Go200 CD.

Let's Learn PUNCTUATION

? wèn hào
问号
(question mark)

When asking a question, a question mark "?" must be added to the end of the sentence.

请问现在几点钟？

dǎ qiú
明天一起去打球，好不好？

! tàn hào
叹号
(exclamation point)

When expressing surprise, anger, excitement, and so on, an exclamation point "!" should be added to the end of the sentence.

tiān   lán   yún bái   tiān qì
天是蓝的，云是白的，天气很好！

早上，我看到王老师，我说："王老师早！"

⭐ Practice It

Fill in the blanks with the correct punctuation marks.

① 前面有车子☐小心☐

wán   yóu xì
② 你要玩什么游戏☐

Let's READ

⭐ Text 1 💿 Go 200

Read the following text carefully.

lán tiān **dui** bái yún
蓝天对白云说："走路要**小心**!"

bái yún **dui** lán tiān   **tiān   hen da**
白云对蓝天说："天很大，

nong
没有红灯，也没有绿灯，

我可以上上下下走，

wán yóu xì
前前后后玩游戏。"

Answer these questions in Chinese.

1 What did the blue sky say?   走路要小心
2 What did the white cloud say? 天很大
3 Can you behave like the white cloud when you are walking on the road? Why or why not?

我不可以上上下下走

Text 2

Read the following text carefully.

今天天气很好，天是蓝的，云是白的。

我看到草地上有很多人，有的在打球，有的在散步，有的在玩游戏。

姐姐和妹妹一起在草地上散步。姐姐戴黑帽子，妹妹戴红帽子。

我在草地上看书，哥哥在草地上打球。弟弟问我："我们也去打球，好不好？"

今天天气很好，大家都很开心。

Answer these questions in Chinese.

1 What is everybody doing on the grass?
2 What colors are the elder and younger sisters' hats?
3 Who asked the author to play a game of ball?

有很多人，有的在散步，有的在玩
姐姐戴 帽子，妹妹戴
红帽子

Go 200

WANT TO LEARN MORE?

Check out the Text > Reading section in the Go200 CD.

Carry out the following dialogue to find out the activities your friends do on Sunday, and if they enjoy these activities. Fill in the table below with the names of your friends and the activities that they enjoy.

Ⓐ: 星期日你要做什么？

Ⓑ: 我和哥哥一起在草地上打球。
cǎo dì　dǎ qiú

Ⓐ: 你爱打球吗？
ài dǎ qiú

Ⓑ: 我爱打球。
ài dǎ qiú

姓名	打球	散步	用电脑	看书	Others
1					
2					
3					
4					
5					

LEARNING LOG

I can...

		Excellent	Good	Fair	Needs Improvement
1	describe objects with the colors "红", "绿", "蓝", "黑", and "白".	☐	☐	☐	☐
2	talk about some common activities such as ball games, strolling, and games.	☐	☐	☐	☐
3	use "好不好？" to seek the opinion of others.	☐	☐	☐	☐
4	use "在……上" and "在……里" to describe the location of an activity.	☐	☐	☐	☐
5	use "？" at the end of a question, and "！" at the end of an exclamation.	☐	☐	☐	☐
6	write "云", "草", "地", "玩", and "球".	☐	☐	☐	☐

春夏秋冬
The Four Seasons

My Goals

1 Describe the sceneries of the four seasons
2 Describe common activities that take place in different seasons
3 Understand how some Chinese characters evolved from illustrations
4 Indicate that two or more different items are in a particular location, or in the possession of someone
5 Become familiar with vocabulary associated with the four seasons and their related activities

huā
花

zhòng huā
种花 (plant flower)

cǎo
草

chú cǎo
除草 (weed)

Think and Answer

What seasons come to your mind when you look at these pictures?

yè zi
叶子

luò yè
落叶

sǎo luò yè
扫落叶 (sweep fallen leaves)

xuě
雪

xià xuě
下雪 (snowing)

chǎn xuě
铲雪 (shovel snow)

New Words

huā 花 flower	cǎo 草 grass	yè zi 叶子 leaf	luò yè 落叶 fallen leaves	xuě 雪 snow

Let's CHANT Go 200

chūn tiān dào le   zhòng huā
春天到了要种花，

xià tiān dào le yào chú cǎo
夏天到了要除草，

qiū tiān dào le sǎo luò yè
秋天到了扫落叶，

dōng tiān dào le yào chǎn xuě
冬天到了要铲雪。

TIP

China depended largely on agriculture, and since some 3000 years ago, has devised a system of spring-ploughing, summer-weeding, fall-harvesting, and winter-storing, which the lunar calendar is based on. Harvesting and storing in fall and winter signified the end of a work year for the farmers, and they welcomed the new year by replacing the old with the new. Till today, the tradition of celebrating the Lunar New Year is practiced by all Chinese. The Lunar New Year occurs approximately between January and February of the Gregorian calendar.

New Words

chūn tiān	zhòng huā	xià tiān	chú cǎo
春天 spring	种花 plant flowers	夏天 summer	除草 weed
qiū tiān	sǎo	dōng tiān	chǎn xuě
秋天 fall	扫 sweep	冬天 winter	铲雪 shovel snow

Let's Learn GRAMMAR

chūn tiān 春天到了，		zhòng huā 妈妈种花，		zhòng huā 弟弟种花。
dōng tiān 冬天到了，	有时	chǎn xuě 爸爸铲雪，	有时	chǎn xuě 姐姐铲雪。

yè zi luò
叶子落了，有时姐姐扫落叶，有时哥哥扫落叶。

sǎo luò yè

姐姐去上学，有时穿红鞋，有时穿白鞋。

我天天吃早饭，有时吃三明治，有时吃面包。

都

今天，我和弟弟都穿蓝色的鞋子。

qiū tiān   yè zi   luò yè
秋天，叶子都落了，路上都是落叶。

zhòng huā   zhòng huā
爸爸爱种花，我也爱种花，

zhòng huā
我们都爱种花。

> Here, "也" indicates that both subjects in the sentence enjoy the same thing. "也" has to be placed after the second subject.
>
> "都" means "all". All the subjects which "都" refer to must be placed before it.

chú le
除了……，还有……

chú le
桌子上，除了笔，还有三本书。

chú le
姐姐的鞋子，除了红的，还有白的。

chú le
妹妹的帽子，除了蓝的，还有红的。

xià tiān   chú le
夏天，除了有红花，还有绿草。

New Words

chú le
除了 besides

Go200

WANT TO LEARN MORE?

Check out the Text > Sentence Pattern section in the Go200 CD.

Find a partner and practice the following dialogues.

⭐ Task 1

A: 春天、夏天、秋天和冬天，你爱哪一个？
　　　 chūn tiān　 xià tiān　 qiū tiān　 dōng tiān　　　　　　　ai

B: 我爱夏天。
　　　 wǒ ai　 xià tiān

A: 夏天你爱做什么？
　　　 xià tiān　　　 ai zuo

B: 夏天我爱在草地上玩游戏。
　　　 xià tiān　　 ai zai　　　　　 you xi

A: 我也爱夏天，夏天我爱在草地上散步。
　　　　　 xià tiān　 xià tiān

⭐ Task 2

A: 我爱秋天，秋天叶子都红了，很好看 (beautiful)。
　　　　　 qiū tiān　 qiū tiān yè zi　　　　　 hǎo kàn

B: 秋天到了，你家有落叶吗？
　　　 qiū tiān　　　　　　 luò yè

A: <u>有，我家有落叶。</u>

B: 秋天谁扫落叶？
　　　 qiū tiān shéi sǎo luò yè

A: 有时 <u>爸爸</u> 扫落叶，有时 <u>我</u> 扫落叶。
　　　　　　 sǎo luò yè　　　　　　 sǎo luò yè

Task 3

A: 你家在哪里？ *zài lí* *里 哪*

B: 我家在新加坡 (Singapore)。 *xīn jiā pō* *every-day*

A: 新加坡会下雪吗？ *xīn jiā pō* *huì* *xià xuě* *ma*

B: 新加坡天天都是夏天，不会下雪。 *xīn jiā pō* *dou* *xià tiān* *xià xuě*

A: 我家在加拿大 (Canada)，加拿大除了夏天， *jiā ná dà* *jiā ná dà chú le xià tiān*
还有春天、秋天和冬天。 *chūn tiān* *qiū tiān* *dōng tiān*
冬天会下雪。 *dōng tiān* *xià xuě*

除了塊还有 *chú le hai you*

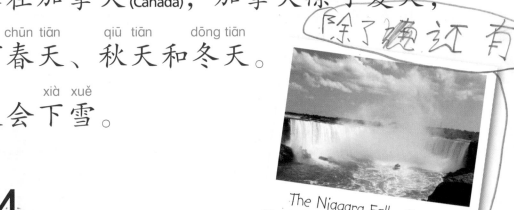

The Niagara Falls, Canada

The Merlion statue, Singapore

Task 4

A: 春天到了，你做什么？ *chūn tiān*

B: 春天到了，我和妈妈一起种花。 *chūn tiān* *zhòng huā*

A: 你们种什么花？ *zhòng* *huā*

B: 除了红色的花，还有白色的花。 *chú le* *huā* *huā*

春夏秋冬 · 91

Task 5

The following dialogue is adapted from the dialogue in your **Go200**. You may listen to the CD before reading the transcript.

Ⓐ: 春天谁种花？
chūn tiān *zhòng huā*

Ⓑ: 妈妈种花，妈妈种很多好看的花。
zhòng huā *zhòng* *hǎo kàn* *huā*

Ⓐ: 夏天谁除草？
xiù tiān *chú cǎo*

Ⓑ: 除了哥哥，还有我，我们都会除草。
chú le *chú cǎo*

Ⓐ: 秋天到了，谁扫落叶？
qiū tiān *sǎo luò yè*

Ⓑ: 哥哥和我扫落叶。
sǎo luò yè

Ⓐ: 冬天谁铲雪？
dōng tiān *chǎn xuě*

Ⓑ: 有时哥哥铲雪，有时我铲雪。
chǎn xuě *chǎn xuě*

Go200

WANT TO LEARN MORE?

Check out the Text > Dialogue section in the Go200 CD.

Let's Learn CHARACTER

⭐ Origin of Chinese Characters

Many Chinese characters evolved from illustrations. Look at the examples below. Can you tell what character each of the following illustrations has evolved into? Write it down.

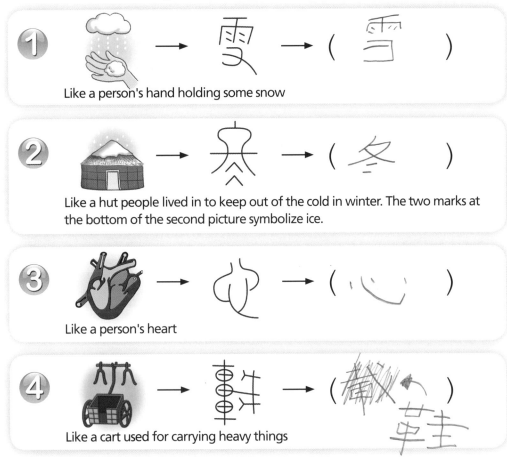

① Like a person's hand holding some snow → 雪 → (雪)

② Like a hut people lived in to keep out of the cold in winter. The two marks at the bottom of the second picture symbolize ice. → (冬)

③ Like a person's heart → (心)

④ Like a cart used for carrying heavy things → (鞋)

⭐ Structure of Chinese Characters

Light Top Component and Heavy Bottom Component

Many Chinese characters are made up of a top component and a bottom component. In some characters, the top and bottom components are proportionate to each other while in others, they are not. This lesson introduces you to some characters with a light top component and a heavy bottom component.

huā 花   luò 落   答

Let's READ

Read the following text carefully.

chūn tiān　　　　　　　　　　huā　kāi
春天，草地绿了，花也开*了。

xià tiān
夏天，草地上有很多人，

有的打球，有的玩游戏。

qiū tiān　　yè　zi　luò
秋天，叶子落了，

zhè　lǐ　　luò　yè　　nà　lǐ　　　luò　yè
这里*是落叶，那里*也是落叶。

dōng tiān　　xià xuě
冬天，下雪了，草地都白了，

　　　　huā　　　　　　　cǎo
看不见花，看不见草，也看不

luò　yè
见落叶。

TIP

What is the difference between "看不见" and "没看见"?

"看不见" means you have taken a look at something/some place but cannot physically see what you want to see due to personal reasons (eyesight or height) or external reasons (somebody blocking you in front, an unclear object, etc.). The negative tag "不" must be placed in the middle of the phrase "看见". In the text, the author cannot see flowers, grass or fallen leaves because it is winter.

"没看见" means you have taken a look at something/some place, but did not see what you were looking for. For example:

A：你看见那个字了吗？
B：我没看见。

* 开 bloom

* 这里 here

* 那里 there

Answer these questions in Chinese.

1 In which season do flowers bloom and grass turns green?

在春天

2 What does "这里是落叶，那里也是落叶" mean?
leaves everywhere

3 According to the text, why is the ground white in winter?
It snows. *下雪了*

★ Text 2

Read the following text carefully.

chūn tiān   huā   kāi   *Bloom*   huā

春天到了，花都开了，我和姐姐去看花。

xià tiān

夏天到了，草都绿了，妹妹爱在草地上玩游戏，

qiū tiān   yè   zi

爸爸和哥哥爱在草地上打球。秋天到了，叶子

yè   zi   hǎo kàn   dōng tiān

都红了，红红的叶子很好看。冬天到了，草地

xuě dì   xuě rén

都白了，我们爱在雪地*上做雪人*。

* 雪地 ground covered in snow

* 雪人 snowman

Complete the table below with the information from the text above. Place a "—" in the table for any information not available from the text.

Season	People Involved	Location	Action
春天	我和姐姐	—	看花
夏天	妹妹爸爸哥哥	草地上	玩游戏,打球
秋天	—	—	很好看
冬天	我们	草地白了 雪地	看 雪人

Go 200

WANT TO LEARN MORE?

Check out the Text > Reading section in the Go200 CD.

Let's DO IT

1 In groups of three, do a recital of this lesson's "Let's Chant".

2 After a group's recital, each student in that group selects a phrase from each of the four categories below to complete this sentence "(When) 到了，我和 (Whom) 在(Where) (What)。"

3 Other students give a round of applause if the student forms the sentence correctly.

4 Each group must complete all of the above steps before another group can proceed.

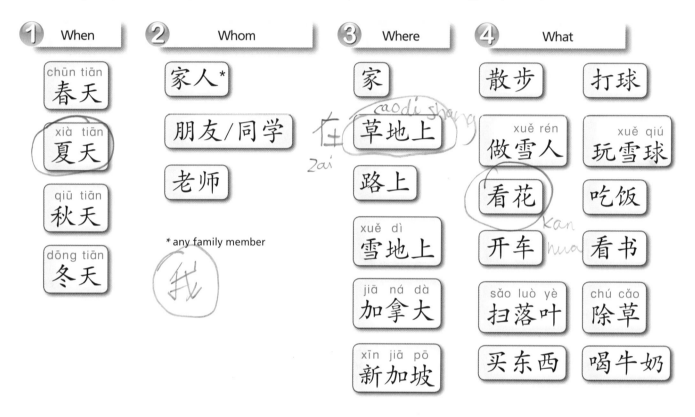

① When

chūn tiān
春天

xià tiān
夏天

qiū tiān
秋天

dōng tiān
冬天

② Whom

家人*

朋友/同学

老师

* any family member

我

③ Where

家

在 草地上
zai   caodi shang

路上

xuě dì
雪地上

jiā ná dà
加拿大

xīn jiā pō
新加坡

④ What

散步

打球

xuě rén
做雪人

xuě qiú
玩雪球

看花
Kan hua

吃饭

开车

看书

sǎo luò yè
扫落叶

chú cǎo
除草

买东西

喝牛奶

I can...

	Excellent	Good	Fair	Needs Improvement
1 state the four seasons in Chinese.	☐	☐	☐	☐
2 describe the scenery and typical activities of each season.	☐	☐	☐	☐
3 use "有时……，有时……", "除了……，还有……", and "都" appropriately.	☐	☐	☐	☐
4 explain how "雪", "冬", "心", and "车" have evolved from illustrations.	☐	☐	☐	☐
5 write "春", "夏", "秋", "冬", and "扫".	☐	☐	☐	☐

我的妈妈
My Mother

My Goals

1. Name the common household chores in my home and state who does them
2. State my perspective on things around me
3. Describe the multiple things that a person has to do
4. Understand the principle of writing the left-falling stroke before the right-falling stroke in Chinese
5. Become familiar with vocabulary associated with household chores

yī fu
衣服

xǐ yī fu
洗衣服 (wash clothes)

yī fu
穿衣服 (wear clothes)

菜

买菜 (buy vegetables or groceries)

zuò cài
做菜 (cook)

字

xiě zì
写字

打字

gōng kè
功课

gōng kè
做功课 (do homework)

★ Answer and Act

Your teacher will state a noun. You have to repeat it with the appropriate verb in the form "verb + noun", and then act out the action. For example:

➤ Teacher: yī fu 衣服。

➤ Student: xǐ yī fu 洗衣服。 (does action of washing clothes)

New Words

yī fu 衣服 clothes	xǐ 洗 wash	xiě zì 写字 write	gōng kè 功课 homework

妈

Let's CHANT Go 200

wǒ de mā ma zhēn xīn kǔ
我的妈妈真辛苦，

zuò fàn xǐ yī fu
买菜做饭洗衣服，
wash

gōng kè
还要教我做功课，

zhēn xìng fú
我有妈妈真幸福。

New Words

zhēn
真 really

xīn kǔ
辛苦 painstaking

zuò fàn
做饭 cook
a meal

xìng fú
幸福 happiness

Let's Learn GRAMMAR

_{zhēn}
真 *really*

TIP

"真" is an adverb used to modify adjectives to give them a greater degree of meaning. It also means something is "accurate" and "real".

_{zhēn}
真好看 ➡ 你的帽子真好看。 _{zhēn}

_{zhēn}
真好吃 ➡ 妈妈做的菜真好吃。 _{zhēn}

_{zhēn}
真好喝 ➡ 这杯果汁真好喝。 _{zhēn}

_{zhēn xīn kǔ}
真辛苦 ➡ 妈妈洗衣买菜真辛苦。 _{zhēn xīn kǔ}

_{zhēn xìng fú}
真幸福 ➡ 我可以上学真幸福。 _{zhēn xìng fú}

TIP

"好" may be used with verbs related to our senses such as "看", "吃", "喝", "听", etc. to form adjectives. For example:
➤ "好看" beautiful
➤ "好吃" delicious
➤ "好喝" tasty (to drink)
➤ "好听" pleasant to hear

好了吗？

Ⓐ: 你扫好了吗？

Ⓑ: 还没，我还没扫好。

Ⓐ: 他洗好了吗？ _{xǐ}

Ⓑ: 还没，他还没洗好。 _{xǐ}

		xǐ yī fu		zuò fàn
姐姐	要	洗衣服，	还要	做饭。
我 *Wǒ*	要 *Yǎo*	学中文，*xué zhong wen*	还要 *hài Yǎo*	学电脑 *xué Dian nao*

我要穿鞋子，还要戴帽子。
chuan xie zi — *Dai mao zi*

我要做功课，还要扫地 (sweep the floor)。
zuo gōng kè — *sǎo dì*

妈妈要做家事 (household chores)，还要教我
zuo jiā shì — *jiao wo*
做功课。
zuo gōng kè

姐姐要买面包，还要买牛奶。

Ⓐ: 你做好了吗？

Ⓑ: 我做好了。

Ⓐ: 弟弟写好了吗？
xiě

Ⓑ: 他写好了。
xiě

TIP

"Verb + 好了吗？" is used to ask the other party if the action is completed. Note the difference between an affirmative answer (completed; on page 101) and a negative one (not completed; on page 100).

Go 200

WANT TO LEARN MORE?

Check out the Text > Sentence Pattern section in the Go200 CD.

Find a partner and practice the following dialogues.

⭐ Task 1

Ⓐ : 谁教你中文?

Ⓑ : 妈妈教我中文。

Ⓐ : 你妈妈教你写字吗?

Ⓑ : 妈妈教我写字,还教我做功课。

Ⓐ : 你妈妈真好。

⭐ Task 2

Ⓐ : 你会扫地吗?

Ⓑ : 会,我会扫地。我天天都扫地。

Ⓐ : 你们家谁洗衣服?

Ⓑ : 我姐姐洗衣服。

Ⓐ : 你姐姐真辛苦。

Ⓑ : 我妈妈要买菜做饭,她也很辛苦。

 **Task 3**

Ⓐ: 妈，我们去散步，好不好？

Ⓑ: 我要洗衣服，还要扫地，我要做很多事。
  xǐ yī fu　sǎo dì
  明天再去散步。

Ⓐ: 妈妈，我扫地，你洗衣服。
  sǎo dì　xǐ yī fu

Ⓑ: 好，你扫地，我洗衣服。
  sǎo dì　xǐ yī fu
  等一下，我们一起去散步。

 **Task 4**

Ⓐ: 你今天功课多不多？
  gōng kè

Ⓑ: （我今天功课很多。）
  gōng kè

> In this practice, B may reply with his own answers.

Ⓐ: 你做好了吗？

Ⓑ: （还没，我还没做好。）

The following dialogues can be found in your ⊙ Go200 . You may listen to the CD before reading the transcript on this page.

⭐Task 5

Ⓐ : （你们家）谁买菜？谁做饭 zuò fàn？谁洗衣服 xǐ yī fu？

Ⓑ : 都是我妈妈，她很辛苦 xīn kǔ。

⭐Task 6

Ⓐ : 你今天功课 gōng kè 多不多？

Ⓑ : 我今天功课 gōng kè 不多，可以去打球。

⭐Task 7

Jeff often helps Julie and Tom with their homework. Julie is thinking of inviting Jeff for dinner on his birthday as a way of thanking him.

Tom : 他的生日 shēng rì (birthday) 是哪一天？

Julie : 就是今天。我们一起请他去吃饭 qǐng！

> **TIP**
>
> "请" is used to sound polite. It can also be used as a verb to mean "invite". A typical sentence structure of this usage is:
>
> | 请 | person invited | activity the person is invited to do |
> |---|---|---|
> | 请 | 他 | 去吃饭 |

⊙ Go200

WANT TO LEARN MORE?

Check out the Text > Dialogue section in the Go200 CD.

Let's Learn CHARACTER

 ## Sequence of Writing Chinese Characters

Left-falling Stroke Before Right-falling Stroke

When there are left- and right-falling strokes in a character, you should write the left-falling stroke before writing the right-falling one.

 ## Alternative Way to Remember Chinese Characters

Link Characters to Illustrations

Though many Chinese characters evolved from illustrations, not all did. However, you may still use illustrations to help you remember many Chinese characters. The following are some good examples of how you can do so.

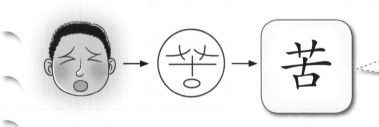

Doesn't this boy look like he is in pain? "苦" means "hardship", so it is often paired up with other characters that also suggest "hardship and suffering", such as "辛苦".

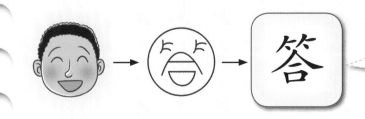

When one is very confident in answering a question, he looks like this boy with a wide smile on his face. It also looks like there is a letter "A" on the face, which you can use to link to the word "answer".

Read the following text carefully.

我有眼睛，可以看天*，看地，看花，
看草。

我有耳朵，可以听你说，听他说，
听大家说。

我有嘴，可以吃这个，喝那个，
还可以说这个，说那个。

我有手，可以做事、拿菜*、打球、
写字，还可以玩游戏；这就是幸福。

* 天 sky

* 拿菜 serve (myself or others) dishes

Answer these questions in Chinese.

1　What does the author say he can see with his eyes?
2　What does the author say he can hear with his ears?
3　What does the author say he can do with his hands?
4　Does the author feel happy? Why?

 **Text 2**

Read the following text carefully.

　　早上，妈妈要做早饭，还要洗衣服xǐ yī fu。洗好xǐ了衣服yī fu，还要去买菜。

　　下午，我和弟弟一回家，妈妈就教我们做功课gōng kè。

　　晚上，妈妈要做饭zuò fàn，妈妈做的晚饭wǎn fàn*很好吃，我们都爱吃妈妈做的饭。

　　我有妈妈真幸福zhēnxìng fú，我爱我的妈妈。

*晚饭 dinner

Answer these questions in Chinese.

1　When does Mother go marketing and do the laundry?
2　Who helps Younger Brother with his homework?
3　What does Mother do at home? List them below in the order in which they are done.

Go 200

WANT TO LEARN MORE?

Check out the Text > Reading section in the Go200 CD.

Let's DO IT

1. Form groups of three or four. Each group is to obtain two dice and a coin. For the coin, heads up indicates "to do something"; tails up indicates "not to do something".

2. Everybody takes turns to toss the dice and the coin simultaneously. The numbers on the dice tell you which phrases to pick out from the table below to form a sentence. For example:
   Student A: Coin lands heads up, dice show three and four respectively.
   Student B: Coin lands tails up, dice show five and six respectively.

3. A answers: 我要做功课(3)，要买菜(4)，还要做三明治(3 + 4 = 7)，真辛苦。

   B answers: 饭，我不会做(5)。草，我不会除(6)。
   鞋子，我也不会洗(5 + 6 = 11)。

4. Everybody has to toss the dice and coin at least twice.

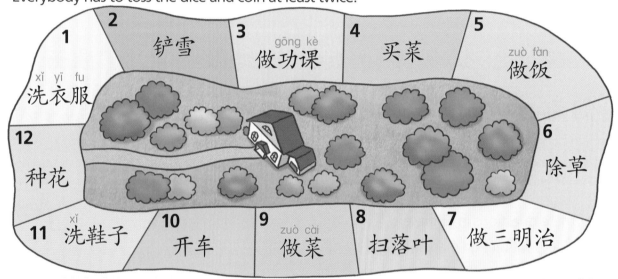

LEARNING LOG

I can...

	Excellent	Good	Fair	Needs Improvement
1 list the common household chores.	☐	☐	☐	☐
2 use "真好看", "真辛苦", "真幸福", and "真好吃" to express my opinion.	☐	☐	☐	☐
3 use "要……，还要……" to describe multiple things that a person has to do.	☐	☐	☐	☐
4 write the left-falling stroke before the right-falling one when they criss-cross in a character.	☐	☐	☐	☐
5 write "真", "洗", "衣", "功", and "课".	☐	☐	☐	☐

我的爸爸
My Father

My Goals

1 Introduce my family

2 State what one can or cannot do, or is disallowed to do

3 Convey a particular time frame in a sentence

4 Understand the principle of writing the radical "辶" last in characters with it

5 Become familiar with vocabulary associated with how my parents look after my family

Get Started

shàng bān
上班

shàng kè
上课 (go to class)

上学

xià bān
下班

xià kè
下课 (end of class)

fàng xué
放学 (after school)

jiē
接

sòng
送

Say the Opposite

Listen carefully to the Chinese words or phrases that your teacher will recite, and state the opposite of those words or phrases.

New Words

shàng bān 上班 go to work	xià bān 下班 get off work	jiē 接 pick (someone) up	sòng 送 send

Go 200

我的爸爸真能干，
néng gàn

上班赚钱照顾家，
shàng bān zhuàn qián zhào gù

每天从早忙到晚，
měi tiān cóng máng

还要接送我上学。
jiē sòng

New Words

néng gàn 能干 capable	*zhuàn qián* 赚钱 earn money	*zhào gù* 照顾 look after
měi tiān 每天 every day	*cóng* 从 from	*máng* 忙 busy

Let's Learn GRAMMAR

弟弟	néng 能 / néng 不能	玩电脑游戏。

TIP "能" affirmatively indicates that one has the capability to do something. "不能" projects a more forceful tone, either indicating that one is incapable of doing something, or that he cannot do it because he is disallowed or hindered by someone/something to do so.

弟弟不做功课，不能去打球。

今天天气不好，我不能去散步。

哥哥能写一百个中文字。

TIP Both "能" and "可以" express permission. However, only "能" can express one's ability to do something.

我	néng 能 / néng néng 能不能	去打球	吗？ / ？

我能去找小明吗？

我能不能去找小明？

我能和你一起去散步吗？

我能不能和你一起去散步？

New Words

néng
能 be able to

cóng
从……到……(time)

cóng　　　　　　　　máng
妈妈从早到晚都很忙。

cóng
我从星期一到星期五都要去
上学。

cóng
哥哥从下午五点到晚上九点都要学电脑。

New Words

yòu
又 again; and

yòu　　　　　yòu
又……，又……

yòu　　　　　　　yòu
爸爸又要扫地，又要做饭。

yòu　　　　　yòu
我又要写字，又要打字。

yòu　　　　　yòu
弟弟又吃饭，又喝牛奶。

yòu　　　　　yòu
这双鞋子又好看，又便宜。

Go 200

WANT TO LEARN MORE?

Check out the Text > Sentence Pattern section in the Go200 CD.

Find a partner and practice the following dialogues.

⭐ Task 1

Ⓐ: 小方，今天谁送你 上学？
　　　　　　　　sòng

Ⓑ: 今天妈妈送我上学。
　　　　　sòng

Ⓐ: 昨天谁送你上学？
　　　　　sòng

Ⓑ: 昨天爸爸送我上学。
　　　　　sòng

Ⓐ: 你爸爸妈妈送你上学，真幸福！
　　　　　　　sòng

⭐ Task 2

Ⓐ: 你爸爸上班，忙不忙？
　　　　　shàng bān　măng máng

Ⓑ: 我爸爸每天都很忙。
　　　　měi tiān　　　máng

Ⓐ: 他每天几点上班，几点下班？
　　　měi tiān　　shàng bān　jǐdiǎn　xià bān

Ⓑ: 他早上八点上班，晚上七点下班。我爸爸
　　　　　shàng bān　　　　　　　　xià bān
每天从早忙到晚。
měi tiān cóng　máng

★ Task 3

 fàng xué jiē
放学了，谁接你回家？

 爸爸 接我 回家 。

 jiē
你爸爸几点来接你？

 五点半
_____ 。

 jiē
你爸爸开车来接你吗？

 Who shei jiē
对！ 谁接你回家？

 妈妈
_____ 。

 jiē
你妈妈开车来接你吗？

 她走路 来接我
_____ 。

The following dialogues can be found in your  Go 200 . You may listen to the CD before reading the transcript on this page.

Task 4

shàng bān

Ⓐ: 你星期六上班吗？

shàng bān

Ⓑ: 我星期六和星期日都要上班，很辛苦。

painstaking

Task 5

měi tiān   shàng kè   xià kè

Ⓐ: 你每天几点上课？几点下课？

měi tiān   shàng kè   xià kè

Ⓑ: 我每天早上八点半上课，下午三点半下课。

Task 6

sòng   jiē

Ⓐ: 谁送你上学？接你回家？

měi tiān sòng   měi tiān jiē

Ⓑ: 爸爸每天送我上学，妈妈每天接我回家。

Task 7

máng máng

Ⓐ: 你忙不忙？

máng   zhào gù

Ⓑ: 我很忙，我要照顾弟弟妹妹。

 Sequence of Writing Chinese Characters

Writing Radical "辶" Last

In characters with the radical "辶", you should write the component on the right before finishing with the radical "辶" on the left.

sòng

 Structure of Chinese Characters

Heavy Top Component and Light Bottom Component

Many Chinese characters are made up of a top component and a bottom component. In some characters, the top and bottom components are proportionate to each other while in others, they are not. This lesson introduces you to some characters with a heavy top component and a light bottom component.

zhào

Text 1 [Go 200]

Read the following text carefully.

爸爸有一双大手，

他的大手真能干(néng gàn)，能(néng)用电脑，也能(néng)开车。

他的大手真能干(néng gàn)，能(néng)洗衣服，也能(néng)做饭。

他的大手真能干(néng gàn)，夏天除草，冬天铲雪。

他的大手真能干(néng gàn)，天天做事，照顾(zhào gù)我们。

Answer these questions in Chinese.

1 What can Father do with his big hands in summer?
2 What can Father do with his big hands in winter?
3 Which of the tasks mentioned in the text can you perform?

除草

铲雪

我真能干扫落叶 做饭。
会会   和
              和

Read the following text carefully.

néng gàn   shàng bān zhuàn qián zhào gù
我的爸爸真能干，他上班赚钱照顾家。他

zhuàn qián   zhuàn qián
赚钱买菜、买衣服。他赚钱买书、买笔。

měi tiān   sòng   měi tiān
每天早上，爸爸开车送我们去上学。每天

jiē   měi tiān cóng   máng
下午，爸爸开车接我们回家。他每天从早忙到

yòu   shàng bān   yòu   jiē sòng
晚，又要上班，又要接送我们上学，晚上还要

教我做功课。我的爸爸真辛苦。

我有一个好爸爸，真幸福。

Answer these questions in Chinese.

1 Why does Father need to earn money? 赚钱照顾家。

2 What does Father use his car for every day?

3 According to the author, is his father busy? What does he do every day?

2. 接送我们上学

3. 很忙。上到玩

Go200

WANT TO LEARN MORE?

Check out the Text > Reading section in the Go200 CD.

Introduce a member of your family by changing the details accordingly in the passage below.

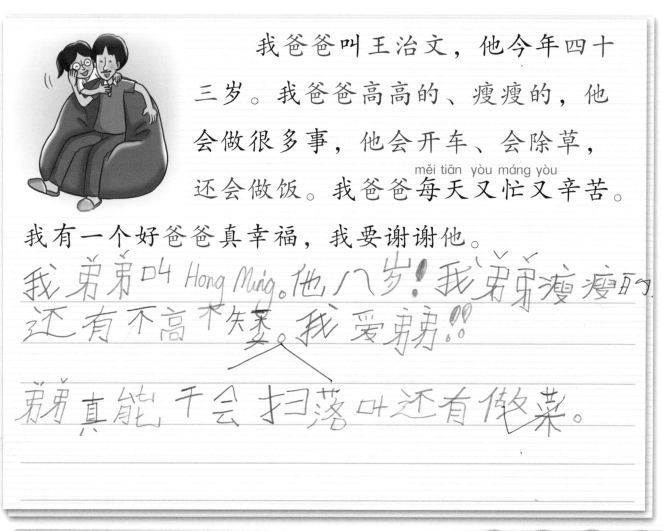

我爸爸叫王治文，他今年四十三岁。我爸爸高高的、瘦瘦的，他会做很多事，他会开车、会除草，还会做饭。我爸爸每天又忙又辛苦。
<ruby>每天 又 忙 又<rt>měi tiān yòu máng yòu</rt></ruby>

我有一个好爸爸真幸福，我要谢谢他。

我弟弟叫 Hong Ming。他八岁！我弟弟瘦瘦的，还有不高不矮。我爱弟弟！！

弟弟真能干会扫落叶还有做菜。

Vocabulary Index

Words indicated with an asterisk (*) are supplementary vocabulary from each lesson. They are included to supplement students' vocabulary and enhance their oral proficiency.

Pinyin	Simplified Character	English	Traditional Character	Lesson
A				
ǎi	矮	short		L3
ài	爱	love	愛	L7
B				
bái sè	白色	white		L7
bái xié	白鞋*	white shoes		L7
bái yún	白云	white cloud	白雲	L7
bái zhǐ	白纸	blank paper	白紙	L2
bāo zi	包子*	steamed bun with stuffing		L5
bēi	背	carry (on the back)		L1
bēi	杯	a cup of (a measure word used for drinks)		L5
bēi bāo	背包	backpack		L1
bēi zi	杯子	cup		L2
běn	本	(a measure word used for books, parts of a series, etc.)		L2
bí zi	鼻子*	nose		L4
bǐ	笔	pen	筆	L2
C				
cài	菜	course (of a meal); vegetable	菜	L5
cǎo	草	grass	草	L8
chá	茶*	tea	茶	L5
chǎn xuě	铲雪	shovel snow	鏟雪	L8
cháng	长	long	長	L3
chē	车*	vehicle	車	L6
chī	吃	eat		L5
chī bǎo	吃饱	eat till one is full	吃飽	L5
chú cǎo	除草	weed	除草	L8
chú le	除了	besides		L8
chuān	穿	wear, dressed in (socks, dress, suit, etc.)		L1
chuān yī fu	穿衣服*	wear clothes		L9

chuáng	床*	bed		L2
chūn tiān	春天	spring		L8
cóng	从	from	從	L10
D				
dǎ qiú	打球	play ball		L7
dǎ zì	打字	type		L4
dài	戴	wear, put on (gloves, accessories, etc.)		L1
diàn nǎo	电脑	computer	電腦	L2
dōng tiān	冬天	winter		L8
duǎn	短	short		L3
duō	多	more		L4
E				
ěr duo	耳朵	ear		L4
F				
fàn	饭	rice; meal	飯	L5
fāng	方	square		L3
fàng xué	放学*	after school	放學	L10
G				
gāo	高	tall		L3
gōng kè	功课	homework	功課	L9
gòu	够	enough	夠	L5
guǒ zhī	果汁	juice		L5
H				
hē	喝	drink		L5
hēi bǐ	黑笔*	black pen	黑筆	L7
hēi mào zi	黑帽子*	black cap		L7
hēi sè	黑色	black		L7
hóng dēng	红灯	red light	紅燈	L6
hóng lǜ dēng	红绿灯*	traffic light	紅綠燈	L6
hóng sè	红色	red	紅色	L7
hóng xié	红鞋*	red shoes	紅鞋	L7
hòu miàn	后面	behind; back	後面	L6
hòu tiān	后天	the day after tomorrow	後天	L7
huā	花	flower	花	L8
huí dá	回答	answer		L2

J				
jiǎo	脚*	foot	腳	L4
jiē	接	pick (someone) up		L10
jiù	就	just		L6
jiù shì	就是	am or is (with added emphasis)		L6
jù zi	句子	sentence		L3
K				
kā fēi	咖啡*	coffee		L5
kāi chē	开车	drive	開車	L6
kàn dào	看到	saw		L3
kàn jiàn	看见	see	看見	L1
kù zi	裤子*	pants	褲子	L1
L				
lán mào zi	蓝帽子*	blue hat	藍帽子	L7
lán sè	蓝色	blue	藍色	L7
lán tiān	蓝天	blue sky	藍天	L7
lǐ	里	inside	裡	L2
liǎn	脸*	face	臉	L4
lǜ cǎo dì	绿草地	green meadow or lawn	綠草地	L7
lǜ dēng	绿灯	green light	綠燈	L6
lǜ sè	绿色	green	綠色	L7
luò yè	落叶	fallen leaves	落葉	L8
M				
mǎi cài	买菜*	buy vegetables or groceries	買菜	L9
máng	忙	busy		L10
mào zi	帽子	hat		L1
měi tiān	每天	every day		L10
miàn	面*	noodles	麵	L5
miàn bāo	面包	bread	麵包	L5
N				
ná	拿	take		L1
néng	能	be able to		L10
néng gàn	能干	capable	能幹	L10
niú nǎi	牛奶	milk		L5
P				
pàng	胖	fat		L3

Q				
qián miàn	前面	front		L6
qián tiān	前天	the day before yesterday		L7
qiū tiān	秋天	fall		L8
qù	去	go to		L1
S				
sàn bù	散步	stroll		L7
sān míng zhì	三明治	sandwich		L5
sǎo	扫	sweep	掃	L8
sǎo luò yè	扫落叶*	sweep fallen leaves	掃落葉	L8
shàng	上	up; above		L3
shàng bān	上班	go to work		L10
shàng kè	上课*	go to class	上課	L10
shàng miàn	上面	on top; above		L6
shàng xué	上学	go to school	上學	L1
shēn tǐ	身体*	body	身體	L4
shēng	声	voice	聲	L1
shǒu	手	hand		L4
shǒu biǎo	手表*	watch	手錶	L1
shǒu tào	手套*	gloves		L1
shòu	瘦	thin		L3
shū	书	book	書	L1
shū bāo	书包	school bag; backpack	書包	L1
shuāng	双	pair	雙	L4
shuō	说	say, speak	說	L1
sòng	送	send		L10
T				
tái	台	(a measure word for computers)		L2
tiān qì	天气	weather	天氣	L7
tīng	听	listen	聽	L4
tíng	停	stop		L6
tóu fa	头发*	hair	頭髮	L4
W				
wà zi	袜子*	socks	襪子	L1

wán	玩	play		L7
wàng	忘	forget		L4
wèn	问	ask	問	L2
wèn tí	问题	question	問題	L2
X				
xǐ	洗	wash		L9
xǐ yī fu	洗衣服*	wash clothes		L9
xià	下	down; under		L3
xià bān	下班	get off work		L10
xià kè	下课*	end of class	下課	L10
xià miàn	下面	under		L6
xià tiān	夏天	summer		L8
xià xuě	下雪*	snowing		L8
xiǎo xīn	小心	be careful		L6
xié	鞋	shoes		L1
xié zi	鞋子*	shoes		L1
xiě zì	写字	write	寫字	L9
xīn kǔ	辛苦	painstaking	辛苦	L9
xìng fú	幸福	happiness		L9
xuě	雪	snow		L8
Y				
yǎn jing	眼睛	eyes		L4
yǎn jìng	眼镜*	glasses	眼鏡	L1
yàngr	样儿	one's appearance; pattern	樣兒	L3
yě	也	also		L5
yè zi	叶子	leaf	葉子	L8
yī fu	衣服	clothes		L1*, L9
yí yàng	一样	the same	一樣	L3
yǐ zi	椅子	chair		L3
yóu xì	游戏	games	遊戲	L7
yòu	又	again; and		L10
yòu	右	right		L6
yòu biān	右边	right side	右邊	L6
yuán	圆	round	圓	L3

Z

zǎo fàn	早饭	breakfast	早飯	L5
zǎo shang	早上	morning		L5
zhāng	张	(a measure word used for flat, sheet-like items)	張	L2
zhào gù	照顾	look after	照顧	L10
zhēn	真	really		L9
zhī	支	(a measure word used for long, thin, inflexible objects)	枝	L2
zhī	只	(a measure word used for one of a pair, or for certain animals)	隻	L4
zhǐ	纸*	paper	紙	L2
zhòng huā	种花	plant flowers	種花	L8
zhuàn qián	赚钱	earn money	賺錢	L10
zhuō zi	桌子	table		L2*, L3
zì	字	word; letter; character		L3
zǒu lù	走路	walk		L6
zuǐ	嘴	mouth		L4
zuǒ	左	left		L6
zuǒ biān	左边	left side	左邊	L6
zuò	做	do		L4
zuò cài	做菜*	cook	做菜	L9
zuò fàn	做饭	cook a meal	做飯	L9
zuò gōng kè	做功课*	do homework	做功課	L9
zuò shì	做事	do something		L4